fellow sunflower lover!

Let your Light Shine!

Deb

Harvest the Bounty of Your Career

DEBORAH F WINDRUM

WITH ARTWORK BY
MICHELE RENÉE LEDOUX

2009

Harvest the Bounty of Your Career
Deborah F Windrum

First Printing

Published in the United States of America by
Axiom Action, LLC
PO Box 3322
Boulder CO 80307-3322
Phone: (303) 499-8120 | Toll-free: (888) 592-4846
Contact for bulk sales: bulk@axiomaction.com
www.AxiomAction.com
Contact the author at www.OMyHarvestMoon.com

Cover Artwork/Design
Michele Renee Ledoux
Fine Artist + Graphic Designer
Email: michele@mledoux.com
www.mledoux.com

Editing
Julia W. Fliss
Co-Founder/Creative Consultant
Art as Endlesss Possibility
Email: julia@artasendlesspossibility.com
www.ArtAsEndlessPossibility.com

Publisher's Cataloging-in-Publication Data
Fink, Deborah, 1949-
Harvest the bounty of your career / by Deb F Windrum;
with art and design by Michele Renée Ledoux.
192 p. 21 cm.
Includes bibliographical references.
ISBN-13   978-0-9801090-2-3
ISBN-10   0-9801090-2-7
1. Career changes. 2. Middle-aged persons—Employment.
3. Middle-aged women—Life skills guides. 4. Self-
actualization (Psychology) in women. I. Ledoux, Michele
Renée. II. Title.
HF5384.F56 2009   650.14
Library of Congress Control Number: 2009922412

Printed in Canada

Axiom Action™

Other books by Axiom Action:
Notes From the Waiting Room: Managing a Loved One's
  End of Life Hospitalization
How to Efficiently Settle the Family Estate

a gift for

from

Thank you

The tree metaphor is an irresistible way to express my appreciation
to those who supported this book to fruition.

To **Susan Anthes** first and foremost—we planted the seed together and cultivated the tender sapling.

My husband, **Bart Windrum**, nourishes and sustains my efforts like a good root system—he actually grocery shops and cooks dinner in addition to providing savvy editorial suggestions and expert publishing services via Axiom Action!

Many wonderful women became the branches of this growing book. Those who participated in pilot workshops and offered invaluable insights. Those who attended other talks and workshops and affirmed the concepts. Those who read an early manuscript and provided considered responses.

My heart-sister **Abbie Loomis** whose thoughtful immersion in the manuscript resulted in a thorough pruning and reshaping that makes this book more sustainable for readers.

You can join me in thanking my editor and "conversational writing" coach, **Julia Fliss**, for the ripening of my academic style to a more palatable fruit for your consumption.

Your experiences as reader are, of course, the seeds this book will release and disperse…

Thank YOU for joining the cycle!

around me the trees stir in their
leaves and call out, "stay a while.
the light flows from their branches,
and they call again, "it's simple,
they say, and you too have come into
this world to do this, to go easy, to be
filled with light, and to shine.

mary oliver

WHAT YOU'LL FIND INSIDE

Welcome

AN INVITATION TO TEA

my story How I discovered my own autumn bounty
and brought this book to fruition

your story What brought you to realize that you are ready
to reap the fruits of your career?

Be patient toward all that is unresolved in your
heart and try to love the questions themselves.
Rainer Maria Rilke

To be happy you must have taken the measure
of your powers, tasted the fruits of your passion,
and learned your place in the world. *Santayana*

We turn not older with years, but new everyday.
Emily Dickenson

Aging forces us to decide what is important in
life. *Thomas Moore*

In any creative process, renewal happens after
we clear the slate. Like our garden, we need to
take some time to rest and reflect on all we have
done, to rejuvenate our minds and our spirits.
As sad as the end of the season is, and as much
as I love the work of gardening, my mind and
body are usually tired by this point, and I relish
the downtime of winter to regenerate myself.
Throughout the cold months, as I inwardly
reflect on what I did this past year and what
I might dream about for next, I think of my
bulbs, snug and secure under the cold earth,
actively resting, too, so they can awaken into
their magnificence come springtime.
Fran Sorin (195)

my story *How I discovered my own autumn bounty*
and brought this book to fruition

If you could come to my home right now, I would greet you at the door with a resounding "Welcome!" and a warm hug. We'd smile, and then I'd guide you to the sliding glass door that overlooks my small yard and the open space beyond. There's a light drizzle this early September day, and I'd want you to see how the abundant fruit on my beloved apple tree are glistening like ornaments. We might feel a bit awkward at first, but I'd put on a kettle of tea, and we'd settle ourselves at a small oak table. We'd pause for a moment to appreciate the nascent autumn hues outside, so pleasingly accentuated by the rain. Isn't it delicious to be cozy inside?

Since you ask, I'll tell you how I discovered my inner autumn bounty and brought this book to fruition...

When I celebrated my fiftieth birthday, I felt youthful, engaged, purposeful. I was confident that I was embarking upon a decade I would find even more fulfilling than my forties, which was a time when I often felt that I was "in my prime." At fifty, I counted among my blessings: health and fitness, a dynamic partnership with my husband, a ten-year-old daughter who fulfilled my somewhat late desire for a child, warm relationships with family members and close friends, an engaging career, a sweet town home in a beautiful location close to hiking trails, and a variety of outlets for self-expression, creativity, and community service.

This satisfaction, however, faded in and out throughout my early fifties as a *dark cloud* began expanding on my horizon. I couldn't believe that the graying hair and sagging chin that showed up in a photograph were really mine. My beloved in-laws were struggling with mounting health issues, and many of my friends were coping with the disabilities and deaths of their parents and in-laws. Suddenly I seemed to be in a hall of mirrors reflecting the diminishments and limitations of old age. "Incredible shrinking elders" seemed to be everywhere. "I don't want to go there" and "What's the point?" I started moaning.

By the time I was into my fifties, I had been an academic librarian for about 25 years. As a junior librarian, I had taken great pride in my rapidly expanding knowledge and in staying at the forefront of my field. By the early 1990s, librarianship was accelerating at a dizzying rate that still has not slowed to this day. However, some years into the 21st century, I started noticing that I was less enthusiastic about keeping pace with the ceaseless tide of new developments. I had to admit to myself that I was no longer riding the crest of my profession. I found it even more disturbing that those just joining the profession seemed to be eyeing me with the same dubious skepticism with which I had once perceived my now-retired seniors. I began to wonder if it was my professional duty to make way for a new wave.

When this metaphor occurred to me, I pictured a wave and realized that the very small portion that is the crest would not even exist, let alone acquire its height, without the much larger and momentum-providing base of the wave. This suggested to me that I was not superfluous and that I could reframe the significance of my current contributions to the library as foundational and enabling, if not always cutting edge in the eyes of my "youngers."

I later found reinforcement for this idea in the book *Retire Retirement: Career Strategies for the Boomer Generation*. The author, Tamara Erickson, says that workers of the Baby Boom Generation might consider enhancing the work life of Generation X employees by "getting out of the way gracefully—with Boomers moving perhaps into individual contributor roles within corporations and turning the reins of leadership over to the Xers" (25). I was pleased to recognize that, in fact, this was exactly how I was approaching my opportunity to have as an assistant an exceptionally bright and capable Gen Xer—allowing him to make choices about what tasks he preferred to take on within our small department and how he would handle them. That he was going to library school and thriving as an up and coming staff member of the library seemed to confirm my satisfaction.

After years of feeling dampened by the dark cloud, I decided to find meaning and value in becoming an "elder." As a positive, future-oriented person who revels in the expansion of self, I still wanted "the best…yet to be." And, since I know Nature is never wrong, I became convinced that aging therefore must not only be natural and appropriate but also hold some benefit, some value. So, I looked to Nature for some deeper sense of the meaning of growth, change, decline, and death. I also starting reading the books listed in the bibliography of this book. I was moved and inspired first by *From Age-ing to Sage-ing: A Profound New Vision of Growing Older* by Zalman Schachter-Shalomi and Ronald S. Miller and especially by *The Second Half of Life: Opening the Eight Gates of Wisdom* by Angeles Arrien.

From Age-ing to Sage-ing includes the biblical representation of life as seven-year periods, each corresponding to a month of the year, so that ages 0-6 is January, 7-13 is February, and so on until 77-?? is December. I found my self, then age 55, positioned late in the month of August and about to commence September and the "autumn" of my life. I was thrilled, as September has always been my favorite month and autumn my favorite season. Viewed as four seasons, the life journey took on new meaning for me.

One dreary winter day, I sought warmth in a hot mineral pool within a dark, narrow cave in Idaho Springs. Floating naked and breathing slowly, I imagined the deep comfort of a womb. It was suddenly clear to me that my first fifty years had been a gestation period, in which I was adjusting to and learning about my own physical self and physical reality. Now floating effortlessly up and down as my breath expanded and contracted, I reflected upon the weight of time, space, and matter. It was in that precise moment that I knew that this decade of my fifties offered the opportunity to birth my spirit, ever weightless and ageless, into a new radiant self.

And I perceived winter, which so feels like an end or a death, as simply one facet of a cycle—as much a beginning as an end and as necessary, beautiful, and inspiring as any other season. So, too, the winter of life—whether called old age, elderhood or any other name—can be embraced as necessary, beautiful, and inspiring. I realized that aging is not a dirty trick of nature, but a journey into wholeness and completeness. Soon thereafter, I found myself energized at the library, and I began relishing the bounty of the autumn season of my life.

I was also inspired to enhance my post-menopausal professional "fitness." My colleagues Susan Anthes, Sue Williams and I began exploring books on memory skills. We created a professional workshop called "Memory Magic," billing ourselves as the memory mavens. We also discussed among ourselves the meaning and value of institutional memory as well as what else might be our most important contributions in this latter stage of our careers.

To develop our concept of institutional memory, Susan and I asked a group of women, now meeting monthly to discuss "Revitalizing Our Vital Years," to brainstorm with us on what the term evoked for them. One of the women tossed out the word "roots." Some months later, when Susan and I took a weekend retreat to develop content for our then working title, *Harvesting the Autumn of Your Career*, we were captivated by the word "roots," from which sprouted the tree metaphor—focusing on roots, branches, fruits, and seeds—that became the genesis of this book.

The book was initiated with the intention of addressing women in the "autumn" of life and latter stages of a career before retirement. As Susan and I piloted workshops and shared excerpts and materials from the developing manuscript, we recognized a more general usefulness of our approach for anyone looking to transition from a career to a next career or stage of life—regardless of time of life or age. Every transition in life can be supported and enriched by the bounty of all that precedes it—the experiences, learnings, gains, releases, relationships and emotions.

After Susan reluctantly withdrew from our collaboration because of professional and personal time pressures, I changed the word "autumn" in the title to "bounty" to include career women of any age who are contemplating any career change. I address women in particular simply because I feel I know women better than men, and because I assume that the process of inner reflection that this book is intended to support is more likely to be embraced by women than men. Having said that, I don't wish to exclude or discourage men from these pages, and I would be delighted to hear from or about men who do find this process useful.

I'd also like to note that I am a recovering academic. I was trained in and my former published writings all personify the impersonal, objective, and intellectual. This book for me is a new foray into the heart-based and personal, but you will find my attention to words and attraction to the heady still very apparent. I think you will also find, however, that the metaphor speaks directly to the heart.

So, now that you know how I came to write this book, I want to know how you came to read this book. Let me freshen our teacups, and then it's my turn to listen. This journey is now about YOU!

your story *What brought you to realize that you are ready to reap the fruits of your career?*

How is it that you came to be reading these pages? Did the book's cover call to you from a bookstore shelf or a friend's dining table? Did someone recommend this book in response to something you said? Were you looking for a book on retirement, career change, or women in midlife? Look deeper and further back in time—what subtle and profound shifts in your experiences as a career woman can you identify as you now focus on them? Have there been changes in your energy, attitude, satisfaction, or desires? Is your interest in change prompted by your chronological age, number of years in your profession, recognition of talents not yet developed or opportunities not yet seized?

Before you begin the next chapter, which offers an overview of what you will find inside this book, I encourage you to create some time and space to look inside yourself. Recall the journey that brought you to and through your career. Reminisce about some of the highlights and trace the contours of your path in your mind's eye. As you do so, be open to the idea that we can imaginatively experience our past as well as our future and that each is a reflection of the other. Know that what we create in our imagination provides a blueprint for the future. Throughout this book, you are invited to enter your imagination and experience your self as a tree and as each part of a tree. You are invited to remember and imagine your self, your journey, your developing life story. You are invited to make this book your own.

Harvest the Bounty of Your Career is about you. It provides a process for you to review, reflect upon, and make discoveries about your life to date, especially your career. Use this book to launch a fresh perspective so you can enhance or change your current work experience or set up a segue into a new endeavor or perhaps "retirement." In this way, you can deliberately optimize the latter stage of a career and initiate a transition to a satisfying next step—whatever that may be for you.

And, now that we've enjoyed our tea, I trust you will take great pleasure in harvesting the bounty of *your* career. Imagine the possibilities as you explore the seasons and cycles of your life, cultivate personal and professional development in the present season, and position stepping stones towards an emerging future of your conscious choice!

> You will become clear only when you look into your heart. Who looks outside, dreams. Who looks inside, awakens. *Carl Jung*

SEPTEMBER 2008

the bounty
OF YOUR CAREER

surveying the wordscape Ideas, terms, and questions
to start your journey

mapping the approach How this book guides you
into new terrain

There is a harmony
In autumn, and a lustre in its sky,
Which through the summer is not heard or seen,
As if it could not be, as if it had not been!
Percy Bysshe Shelley

… the best is autumn.
It is mature, reasonable and serious, it glows
moderately and not frivolously … It cools down,
clears up, makes you reasonable … *Valentin*

The season for enjoying the fullness of life—
partaking of the harvest,
sharing the harvest with others, and reinvesting
and saving portions
of the harvest for yet another season of growth.
Denis Waitley

Autumn is the eternal corrective. It is ripeness
and color and a time of maturity;
but it is also breadth, and depth, and distance.
What man can stand with autumn
on a hilltop and fail to see the span of his world
and the meaning of the rolling
hills that reach to the far horizon? *Hal Borland*

Change is a measure of time and, in the autumn,
time seems speeded up. What was is not and
never again will be; what is is change.
Edwin Teale

The highest reward for a person's toil is not what
they get for it, but what they become by it.
John Ruskin

surveying the wordscape Ideas, terms, and questions
to start your journey

A definition of "career"

Let's start with a clarification of some of the basic concepts we will address in this book.

I use the word career broadly to describe employment, or any endeavor you consider focused and informing work, that requires at least some college education and/or advanced training; includes some degree of responsibility beyond fulfillment of specific, assigned tasks; and involves some level of professional development. To me, a professional is one who manifests respect for her self and her work, feels pride in performance, and holds a view of the job or organization larger than her own duties. In my mind, "professionalism" is less about qualifications and more about qualities and attitude. For many women, a profession or career may mean much more than a livelihood and may be experienced as a "calling."

For that matter, you may be a homemaker or caretaker, self-employed in the home or as a consultant, a job-changer, or holder of any number of "non-traditional" designations or occupations that have shaped your life and manifested as a "career" for *your* intents and purposes. Perhaps you have not walked a straight, ascending, or otherwise socially acknowledged path. It is not unusual for a woman's work life to be pieced together into a "crazy" quilt or woven into a beautiful tapestry from many coordinated fibers and threads. While men often climb a prefabricated ladder, many women discover instead the integrity of a waveform, spiral, or circle.

If you trace a line that reflects your "professional" form, what shape does it find or suggest? How have you chosen to experience this form? How would you *like* to experience it? As much as the choice to experience your professional form is yours, so is the choice to experience this book.

Harvest the Bounty of Your Career is about and for *you*—you decide if you can profitably address a traditional career or any extended period of time dedicated to focused and informing work.

For simplicity, I will use the term "workplace" to refer to the location where your work did, does, or will take place.

The meaning of a career

Young women today may take for granted that they have a range of opportunities and ease of access to careers. To better reflect upon the meaning of your career, it may be useful to remember for a moment the not-very-distant struggles and enormous gains represented by the current, comparatively diverse, options.

Before the 19th century, legitimate "careers" were available primarily to men in the military, clerical, medical, and legal professions. A few determined women became teachers, writers, singers, and even doctors and lawyers. However, most women who were required to earn a living were prostitutes, midwives, herbalists, caretakers, seamstresses, or domestic workers—occupations that offered no formal education or training, status, or upward mobility. The concept of a career as we know it today developed over the course of the 20th century as a result of expanded educational opportunities, challenged social conventions and mores, and the rise of corporations. As a result of the 1940s war effort, American women entered the workforce and a wider range of jobs in unprecedented numbers and often with great fervor. After the war, they surged into higher education, further broadening skills and opportunities. By 2004, according to the U.S. Department of Labor, almost 60% of women were in the labor force, and "half of all management, professional, and related occupations were held by women" (1).

Entering into and fulfilling a career may hold different meanings and implications for a woman than a man. Not only because the role of career woman is a recent historical phenomenon and the culmination of social activism, but also because it is still typically combined with child bearing and often with primary responsibility for child rearing and homemaking. A woman's aspiration for a career is as likely to arise from a felt imperative for social engagement and personal fulfillment as it is from a need for a higher standard of living or status. And yet, women are less likely than men to become entirely identified with their profession or career, and more likely to resonate with the opportunities change provides for redefining and reinventing their self-image and approach to life. In *Retiring as a Career*, Betsy Kyte Newman says, "…this need to adjust or recreate our self-image is among the most crucial of the psychological, emotional, and spiritual needs of retirement" (61). The same need holds true when we change careers.

The decision to leave or retire from a salaried position can be among the most significant of life choices. An employer provides structure, security, constraints, and benefits. Whether we are in service to a profession, organization, or paycheck, our lives are regulated by our employment, not unlike the regulation provided by parents and schools in our youth. For example, our work schedule is likely to determine when we arise in the morning, perhaps even when we eat, and probably when we enjoy leisure. We are typically dependent upon our employer for health care and retirement options. Consider what elements of parental control and safety are present in your working situation. What will it mean to take more control of your life outside the parameters of employment?

One of the consequences of being part of any particular organization is that you are likely to find yourself in some degree of compromise with your "authentic" self. Have you simply adapted to requirements that may not be in keeping with your personal preferences, such as an 8 to 5 weekday schedule? Or, has your approach included becoming a crusader for issues such as flexible scheduling or others that are meaningful to you? Perhaps neither a stance of compliance or resistance is a natural one for you. It will be a major shift, then, to experience life as a "free agent," completely responsible for your time, your days, your self, your life. This book will assist you in exploring the ramifications of such a choice and in considering all that may be gained and therefore embraced as well as all that may be lost and therefore appreciated as a result of such a choice.

How different would your life be had you not dedicated the time and energy thus far in the development of one or more endeavors that you would describe as a career? How different would your personal identity be without the context of a career? To what extent has your life and your sense of self been shaped by a career? What have been the rewards and sacrifices? How will your current choices and your future be determined by your career?

What is the "bounty" of a career?

Anyone who has invested significant time, energy, and life resources in a work endeavor has also endowed her own self with a largess of experience, skills, knowledge, perspective, and discernment—the personal bounty of your career. The bounty is a complex of results and outcomes, both more inner or personally felt and more outer or socially recognized by others. Although results include accomplishments and achievements, more privately noted outcomes that are personally life enhancing are especially significant. We will specifically address such "legacies" in the Fruits chapter, and you will become aware of a rich bounty in every other chapter as well. In the final chapter, "Your Harvest," you will discover how the ultimate inner bounty of your career surpasses the sum of each part considered in turn.

Since the "bounty" we are speaking of is both the parts and the whole of all the seasons that brought you to your current autumn, this book offers an opportunity to reap your professional bounty and create life change whether you are experiencing a season of autumn because you consider yourself in *the* autumn of life chronologically or *an* autumn of life circumstantially.

"An autumn" vs. "The Autumn" of life

Have you noticed how seasons and the course of human lives are often intertwined? Each season each year stimulates and influences our life in ways both subtle and profound. How many decisions and desires in your life have been affected by the time of year? How many times has your state of mind or very life shifted as the season changed?

We also experience many seasons within our lives—times when we feel as fresh as spring, energetic as summer, or bereft as winter. New beginnings may evoke a spring-like state and transitions may signal an autumn of life, regardless of the month indicated by the calendar. If you are contemplating a career change or retirement, you are likely to precipitate an autumn in your life— an opportunity to harvest the bounty of your career and appreciate the potential of change.

Throughout every year of our lives, nature shows us patterns and offers gifts by completing the cycle of seasons and providing many opportunities to learn about and appreciate completing our own life cycle. And, every new stage and development of life embodies the complete cycle of seasons— that is, a beginning, developmental period, maturation period, and rest. Although this book is about experiencing life from the perspective of a personal autumn, you will still continue to recycle through springs, summers, autumns and winters in your life as well as in nature.

At any point in our chronological life, we may have urges, emotions, and experiences that harken to qualities of any season. We all know the energizing rush of fresh new possibilities—that sense of sparkling, dancing, joyous beginning—ah, spring! Think of your expansive times of growth and maturation—so busy, so fruitful—life is heating up! And the abundance and fulfillment, the quickening and quieting of harvest times—bountiful transition! Do you also savor those times of inner movement—the deep and still—bracing cold, restful dark?

And, just as there are spring-like days in winter or wintry days in summer, any period of our chronological life may include sensations or experiences that seem more reflective of a different season. Many maturing women notice an inner youthfulness or timelessness that seems to belie our chronological or socially-perceived age. Some of us find ourselves marrying well after our nubile years, mothering when others our age are grandmothering, or initiating a career as peers retire. Perhaps you had responsibilities during your youth that wouldn't typically be expected until much later in life, or a hysterectomy before your cohort entered perimenopause. Whatever our life course, we may experience urges, desires, and life events that are out of sequence or chronology according to convention.

The situational autumns that spiral throughout our lives are set off by a variety of occurrences, including graduations, moves, new and concluding relationships, marriages, divorces, child birth or adoption, deaths, job and career changes, and fluctuations in income. Even the season itself can catapult us into an autumn in our life. Often, an autumn time in life sparks a life review, whether you are still in life's springtime, summer, or fall. Most of us question our life, values, successes and failures many times during our life. If you are compelled or have chosen to make a change in your career, you may identify with many aspects of the following description of the transition to or through *The* Autumn of a woman's life.

And if you are in The Autumn of life…

Like the season of the year, The Autumn of life (generally early to mid-fifties through mid-to-late seventies) offers opportunities to harvest, clear, evaluate, and prepare for the future. Your health and finances may be such that you are not in a day-to-day survival mode. You may be able to reap the fruits and material security of your labors as a worker. In fact, a hallmark of a late-season career is a potential shift from working for an 'other' because you must insure an income to working for yourself because it remains satisfying on one or more levels or because you choose to maximize your retirement income.

If you enjoy sustainable health, an expectation of longevity, and an income congruent with your needs (if not desires), you have the freedom to explore choices. Regarding employment, you might continue the status quo, reduce your number of hours at work, change responsibilities or type of work, retire early or on schedule, or work beyond a typical retirement age. You may have the resources to make decisions concerning your life style, including type of residence, location, companions, travel, personal enrichment pursuits, or volunteer work. You can also choose options for deliberate growth and development.

Perhaps you have started exploring retirement options or plan to remain in your current position as long as possible. Perhaps you are ready to move on to another type of employment or another endeavor. You may already be retired and wondering what it was all about, whether you made a difference, or what distinguished you and your career. Perhaps you are considering reentering the workforce or starting up your own business.

At this stage of your life, you may be discovering that aging is a lot more fun and satisfying than you expected. Perhaps you are anticipating a second, better half of life or a second chance at life. Maybe you are energized by newly perceived options and opportunities and a sense of freedom and possibility. Perhaps you are eager to pursue some long-awaited vocation, travel, spend more time visiting, or rouse some latent passion. Many women past menopause are refreshed by a sense of rejuvenation and delighted to feel young again, but with the perspective of maturity. This is not just a second adolescence, but our senescence, or passage from adulthood to mature being.

Or you may be finding yourself uncharacteristically restless, irritable, dissatisfied, confused, or filled with some unnamable longing or mysterious yearning. Maybe your current response to your life or the world is not what you expected or hoped for. Perhaps you long for some sort of resolution, clarity, understanding, or closure. Perhaps you find yourself—whether joyfully or uncomfortably— stirred from within to reconsider and redefine priorities and values. Longings to clear, complete, prepare, or dream often mark the transition to The Autumn of life.

The Autumn of life is an opportunity to achieve fulfillment; create closure; clear, prepare, and reclaim; and begin again with experience, foresight, information, knowledge, wisdom, awareness, mindfulness, deliberateness, intention. The transition through an autumn is a time for dreaming, visioning, planning and an opportunity to orchestrate your own 'coming of *next* age' passage.

What circumstances, desires, and inner urgings characterize your current autumn season and perhaps brought you to this book? Or, are you still wondering what season you're in?

What season are you in?

As I revise this section, it is the last week of August. Days are still hot and summery, but there are unmistakable signs of the coming season. Mornings are cooler and evenings darken earlier. More leaves are scattered on lawns, and many of them are golden. When I began this book two years ago, there were signs in my work life indicating the approach of a new season. I realized that few thoughts centered on the library as I drifted to sleep at night or awoke in the mornings. I was simply amused by the earnestness of some committee members and less inclined to fight for an issue. I hadn't attended a professional conference for years. I had become a devoted steward of my energy in all endeavors.

A friend of mine in her early thirties realized her career had phased into an autumn when she noticed that her social life had withered and her young daughter was increasingly frustrated with her absences at dinner. The high-stress career was no longer worth its toll on her personal life. So, she quit and found a more forgiving job.

Since you are reading this book, you are probably aware of indicators of a readiness for change in your own career and life. What are you noticing that represents a change about your feelings, desires, motivations, and expectations? Are you finding yourself more focused on future possibilities than the demands of the present? Perhaps you are increasingly annoyed with aspects of your work or just plain tired. You might benefit by pausing here to jot down a list of shifts in your work experience.

Susan devised a humorous checklist to determine if your current career is turning to an autumn. If your answer is "yes" to one or more of the following questions, this book offers a solution!

1. Are you bored with the same old routines at work? (Are your branches yearning for new and different paths of growth?)
2. Do you have other activities you wish to attend to or spend more time on? (Are there new branches and leaves you would like to grow?)

3. Have your professional efforts grown as far as they can in your current position? (Is the forest encroaching on you in a way that inhibits your growth?)

4. Do you look at work-related concerns with a "historical" perspective? (Are you among the oldest trees in the forest?)

5. Do you feel nudged at work by new or younger staff to adopt new strategies and technologies? (Are fresh, pushy saplings crowding your space?)

6. Do you wonder why it all matters so much to some people? Why they are willing to fight for their position or every little bit of work territory? (Do you wish the noisy nesting creatures would find another tree?)

7. Can you "let go" of issues more readily? (Do you shed old leaves and useless branches with ease?)

8. Are you delegating more? Reluctant to take on new long-term projects? (Are you less concerned about how other trees grow or what the forest becomes?)

9. Do you like being alone more than attending meetings? (Would you rather stare at your own roots than interact with other trees?)

10. Are you more interested in comfort than style? (Are you willing to grow in your own directions and not worry about the usual growth patterns of trees?)

11. Are you finding Being more pleasurable than Doing? (Would you rather just experience the feel of sun or rain on your branches than imagine you can control the elements?)

12. Are people asking if you are leaving or when you will retire? (Are the loggers looking at you as a potential candidate for cutting and thinning of the forest?)

mapping the approach *How this book guides you into new terrain*

If you've decided to pursue harvesting the bounty of your career with this book, you may feel ready to plunge into the following thematic chapters before reading the details surrounding the process and specific organizational patterns that this book sets in motion. If so, go for it and enjoy! You can always come back here to read more about the approach, the organization of the chapters, and how to benefit from the "Acorn" questions and the "Stepping Stones" activities.

On the other hand, if you prefer to start with an overview and know in advance what to expect, this section is just for you...

The Process

When we passage to a new season of life, we typically invest considerable energy in the procedural requirements of the change. Sometimes we are too busy or engrossed to provide commensurate attention to the inner processes and emotional responses that manifest whether they are sufficiently addressed or not. This book will assist you to explicitly process the inner experiences of career change or retirement, which otherwise might occur only implicitly, so that you can create mindfully your own transition to your next season of life.

This book is intended to be useful at any point in your process of concluding or shifting a career and experiencing the "what comes next." If you begin while still working, you may feel empowered to "fulfill" your career and make considered choices about modifying or completing that path. In that case you may find that your transition to a new cycle will emerge naturally and grow organically as a result of your forward-looking process.

If you begin this book after you have transitioned or retired, you may find that your changed circumstances or fresh set of opportunities is an ideal context for engaging in this process. You may discover considerable value in completing some of the activities retrospectively and using other activities to guide you now and in the future.

Like life and learning, this book and the process you will engender is about spiraling. Every time you return to the book or a chapter it will be at a different point in time, following changes and insights in your life—even if minute and mundane—and with a fresh perspective and emergent context. There are many benefits to revisiting sections during your first perusal of the book and beyond. In fact, you can return to any chapter, select a completely different array of activities, and create a completely different experience of the topic.

This book suggests simple processes for pausing briefly to take stock of your inner bounty, appreciate the abundance, and consider a cornucopia of choices for creating a conscious, relevant, and personally satisfying next season of life. This book will guide you to consider your career, but not in terms of successes or failures, good or bad, right or wrong. You will celebrate your career, life, skills, accomplishments, and your unfolding future. You will choose what to notice and to embrace as seeds for a new season.

The Approach

The approach of this book is not formulaic, prescriptive, or a set of ordered steps. Rather, you will find questions and experiences to stimulate reflection, remembering, dreaming, and imagining in order for you to discover your answers within. The questions are *for your consideration*. To *consider* can be a powerful act. "Consider" means to pay attention to, view with care, regard thoughtfully and respectfully; it also means to reflect and honor. Etymologically, the word is derived from the Latin prefix meaning "together with" and the Latin word for "the stars," sidereal. To consider, then, is to align your self with the stars.

What might the stars mean to you in this context—fate, destiny, a fulfilled or realized life, higher knowing, life purpose, the universe? You will decide what to consider and with what your consideration will bring you into greater alignment as you process the questions in this book.

In some instances you may ponder questions in this book; and some may inspire action. Other questions you will simply read, and your reaction or response may occur on an other-than-conscious level. Questions are a powerful tool because the brain responds to them reflexively. That little curved, stemmed, and dotted punctuation mark triggers a cognitive response that continues beyond conscious awareness, sometimes even into your dreams. My intention is to plant seeds that unfold, appropriately and as desired in your mind, heart, and life, to enrich an autumn season and prepare for a new spring.

Rather than a body of text to passively read and then shelve or give away, this book is intended to be a deeply engaging, growing, and spiraling process. The more actively you engage with the material, the more deliberate or intentional your process will be. Even just passively reading this book, however, is likely to stimulate spontaneous or synchronous processing within you. Although functioning largely beneath the surface and unseen, like a root system, the power of metaphor can sustain you as you branch out, flower, discover new fruit, and cultivate your own seeds. If the central tree and seasonal metaphors take root for you, they will support and nourish your growth.

The Activities

Acorns

As mentioned before, each chapter includes many questions throughout the text to engage your own inner process as you read. Each chapter also includes a set of "acorn" questions that will prompt you to distill the essence of the chapter and integrate what nourishes you. Your cumulative answers to the Acorn questions will position you to fully reap your harvest. Your responses then are the seeds from which future growth emerges.

Stepping Stones

The additional exercises, activities, and experiences in each chapter are "stepping stones," that is, markers or placeholders that will ease and sustain your path to a next season and stage. To support you in generating as many possibilities as you desire, each chapter concludes with a variety of Stepping Stones from which you can select those with which you most resonate. It is not necessary to complete all or even most of the options. Just pick any Stepping Stones that most appeal to you. Later, you may find that you wish to select more as the direction and contours of your path materialize. Even if you don't complete any of the exercises, just reading them may stimulate your own ideas for activities that will serve you.

Narrative Journaling

The Stepping Stones for each chapter include narrative journaling activities, which are beneficial in isolation and even more beneficial in combination with other journaling activities and/or other types of experiences. I highly recommend that you acquire a beautiful new journal to enhance your experience. Add to it as you proceed through this book and after. Selecting, personalizing, and starting fresh with special accoutrements marks the value of this endeavor, importance of your commitment, and strength of your intentions. Your investment signals your anticipation, positive expectations, enthusiasm, curiosity, and willingness to be playful and adventurous.

Given the spiraling nature of this process, you may find yourself circling back around to previous chapters to extend or deepen them. On the one hand, you may wish to begin by dividing your physical journal into at least seven sections: To Harvest, Roots, Branches, Fruits, Seeds, My Harvest, A Woman's Life Cycle.

In this way, you will have allocated space for working with each section as you go and as you return. You may want to allocate an additional section for any miscellany, thoughts or ideas that occur to you and don't seem to fit into any categories. Other categories may also suggest themselves to you.

On the other hand, you may prefer a more free-form and organic approach, adding to your journal where and when you are so inspired. This is *your* process, and it will be most enriched by experiencing it as you prefer.

Visual Journaling

Each section also includes guided journaling activities in a form that may be new or uncomfortable for you—visual journaling. Visual journaling is not about creating art or being artistic or exceptionally creative (although it may be that for you). Visual journaling is about using the power of the image, the doodle, the nonlinear, color, form, shape, dimension, intuition, emotion, and free association to tap into your inner mind and heart in a way that is more mysterious, insightful, and profound than the logical, rational, linear written word.

One way to ease into this form of expression and to begin to make it natural and comfortable is to keep your journal at hand while you are reading the chapters of this book (or any book for that matter) and allow yourself to simply pause and doodle from time to time (best with color markers!) as an unstructured means of reflection that stimulates the creative side of your brain. You may find that you can abstractly represent cloudy, formative thoughts even if they are not clear to you in the moment. When you return to your journal after completing the chapter, you may be surprised at what the doodles reveal about your heart/mind process as you initially encountered the material. You may also find that the visual representations of your experience affect your dreams—also a creative-side-of-the-brain function and a form of inner communication.

The more challenged or uncomfortable you are by the idea of putting marker to paper to produce something other than words, the greater the benefit of this choice is likely to be. In *The Artist's Way*, Julia Cameron suggests that you "ask yourself if you can acquire the humility to start something despite your ego's reservations. The grace to be a beginner is always the best prayer for an artist. The beginner's humility and openness lead to exploration. Exploration leads to accomplishment. All of it begins at the beginning, with our first small and scary step" (140).

Again, each visual journaling experience is beneficial in isolation and even more beneficial in combination with other visual journaling activities and/or other types of experiences. If you are captivated by the process of visual journaling, you may wish to acquire a separate blank book (so inspiring!) and a fresh set of markers (so fun!) so as to provide the sacred space your visual journaling process needs to thrive. Whatever combination of journal, notebook, and/or blank book you choose, add to it as you proceed through this book *and after*.

Interpersonal Experiences

The interpersonal experiences offer opportunities to involve someone else in your process, interact informally with others, start a group, receive or offer support. It can be useful for your own process to hear others describe their paths, and there is value in being heard and witnessed. Consider also that sharing some aspect of your own story may be a gift to the listener, who may feel more connected to you, identify with your experience, or find some inspiration for her own situation.

> When someone tells you what they believe, no matter how interested you are, it is natural for some level of disagreement or skepticism to arise, even subconsciously, which is a process of separation. Conversely, when someone, shares their struggles and questions, it is natural for empathy to arise, which is a process of understanding and connection. *Mark L. Tompkins*, (viii)

Workplace Applications

The workplace applications suggest activities, such as report writing or formal mentoring, that are appropriate in the workplace. If you are engaging with this book while you are still in the workplace, your process may help you to clarify your desires and options. It may serve you in creating closure or continuing your legacies. There may be benefits for the workplace in the choices you make or the contributions that are generated.

Notes

Let the format and layout of this book open the door to a new approach for entering and benefiting from a book—just as the intent of this book is to open the door to a new approach for entering and benefiting from the best and most vital decades of your life. I trust that your journey with this book will be enjoyable, thought-provoking, and self-revealing—a process for reaping the legacies of your being and planting the future you envision.

About the examples: I include some of my own experiences throughout as examples. For contrast, I describe situations of "friends" and "colleagues," who are actually just composite characters. They never represent a single or particular person, and they should not be construed as such. The examples are provided for comparison in order to stimulate your own thinking.

About the quotes: I am a lover and collector of inspirational quotes, and I trust they will add to your experience as well. I found many of them in isolation as quotes, and in those instances only an author's or speaker's name is included. In those cases where I extracted a quotation from a text, the author of the quote is followed by a page number, and a full citation for that book can be found in the bibliography.

About experiencing this book with a group: If you are interested in sharing your harvesting process with a small group of friends, find more information in "Experiencing Harvesting in a Group Setting" in the last section, "Continuing Your Journey."

to harvest

awakening *What is prompting you to harvest now?*

envisioning *Using metaphors to harvest and using the tree as metaphor*

What lies behind us and what lies before us are tiny matters compared to what lies within us.
Ralph Waldo Emerson

…the actual task is to integrate the two threads of one's life… the within and the without.
Pierre Teilhard de Chardin

…the consummation of work lies not only in what we have done, but who we have become while accomplishing the task. *David Whyte* (5)

If you want to know your past—look into your present conditions. If you want to know your future—look into your present actions.
Chinese Proverb

Reflection is one of numerous contemplative wisdom practices found in all world traditions. In reflecting, you review, question, and reassess, gaining new insights that may provide you with choices you had not considered before, in order to learn from and integrate your experience.
Angeles Arrien (27)

We do not receive wisdom. We must discover it for ourselves after a journey through the wilderness, which no one else can make for us, which no one can spare us, for our wisdom is in the point of view from which we come at last to regard the world. *Helen Harkness* (*Capitalizing on Career Chaos*, 43)

In old English the word harvest meant the autumn season. By the middle ages, the word came to denote the process of gathering ripe, or, if you will, mature crops.

When seeds that we have planted and tended develop into mature plants and come to fruition, we gather the yield for nourishment and sustenance. The culmination of deliberate growth and development is a return of life-giving energy.

Try rereading the preceding paragraph and imagine that it is a description of your career. As a result of cultivating competencies and knowledge, you became an experienced and proficient—i.e., mature—professional. Your crop of skills and expertise is always available for harvesting. Do you wish the yield of your career now to become merely refuse or memories, or will you choose to return the vital energy cultivated in your field to some greater good that nourishes and sustains your heart and perhaps others?

When we are establishing a life and career, we are in motion, steered by fast-moving currents with precious few opportunities to pause, let alone reflect or renew. A change in direction can be a powerful stimulus to step back or reprioritize in order to contemplate values and desires and to consider choices. The time for reflection that seemed so elusive becomes an imperative. An autumn of your life or career may offer more space to fulfill long-held desires to look within, get to know yourself more deeply, and create more alignment between your inner and outer selves. In retrospect, your past may reveal patterns that illuminate your present and empower you to more deliberately create the future. Are these gifts you would like to provide for yourself now?

Even if you have already left a position in order to enter retirement or make a career change, now is a perfect time to review your career and life. Perhaps you worked steadily right through your very last day on the job, telling yourself that you didn't have time for contemplating unemployment or retirement. You may have felt clear that all you wanted was to simply indulge yourself with more sleep and opportunities to do those things you most enjoy but never found the time to do fully. Did you experience some aversion to any planning, only to wake up weeks, months, or years after retiring to discover that everything had changed more profoundly than you could have imagined?

You still have the opportunity to create a conscious bridge or transition to your next stage. In fact, you may find that you are more effectively able to engage in this process without the pressures of work.

Wherever you are now on a career-change path, you can use this book to renew and restart. You may have the opportunity now—perhaps for the first time in your life—to make choices based on your own innermost promptings rather than on socially imposed or unconsciously internalized motivators, no matter how "honorable" they may have once felt. Often, in our attempts to fulfill outer expectations and social values, we neglect our own deepest urges and heart-felt desires. Would you discern their reflection in the wellspring of your being if, even briefly, you stilled the ripples of your life?

awakening *What is prompting you to harvest now?*

One reason to harvest may be a gnawing or growing sense of restlessness or dissatisfaction. Perhaps your current career no longer serves you in terms of scheduling, mental and/or physical health, values, or finances. Perhaps you have been deeply immersed in your career for a long time, thriving on the challenges, and you are now noticing a lessening of that satisfaction and a longing for more time to engage in other activities.

Many useful books address this turning point. In *When Work Doesn't Work Any More*, Elizabeth Perle McKenna says:

> …there comes a time when the neglected parts of our lives exact a price for this lack of balance. The symptoms range from old-fashioned burnout to boredom, an increasing sense of injustice or just plain old depression. The rewards from work stop compensating for a feeling of emptiness, wasted time, and a decreased sense of purpose and importance. These feelings get worse and worse and must be acknowledged and reckoned with—otherwise they can sour years of accomplishment. Once dissatisfaction sets in, the only remedy is to find some balance between work and the rest of life (11).

Another reason to harvest is to address significant life questions. Many authors emphasize the importance of this pursuit. In *Retiring as a Career* (xiii), Betsy Kyte Newman lists the following "cosmic" questions as typical for more than 50 retirees responding to a 2002 survey:

- Was the life I've lived the one I wanted to live?
- What can I afford to do with it now?
- Did I fulfill my potential?
- Can I still be the person I once wanted to be?
- Who am I now really?
- What kind of relationships do I want and need?

Suzanne Braun Levine, author of *Inventing the Rest of Our Lives: Women in Second Adulthood*, says that for many working women over 50, work is still

> where we find satisfaction, excitement, financial security, and, in part, escape from the personal and family questions that beset us. But, even for us, priorities have changed. Ambition has given way to self-fulfillment; the need for recognition has been replaced by self-assurance, success by achievement, and knowing the ropes by learning new things…. the focus has moved from outside in. From dependence on the environment to dependence on self. Each of us is trying to understand where work fits into the discoveries we are making about who we are now (83).

In *The Second Half of Life*, Angeles Arrien says, "In our later years [we must] look at where we have become over-identified with the roles we have played or the expertise we have developed earlier in life. We begin to clearly see the ways in which we confuse our roles, skills, or professional reputations with who we actually are" (53).

James Hollis, who after twenty years in academia redirected his career to become a Jungian analyst, also comments on this inner transition in *Finding Meaning in the Second Half of Life*:

The relinquishment of ego ambition...will in the end be experienced as a newfound and hitherto unknown abundance. One will be freed from having to do whatever supposedly reinforced one's shaky identity, and then will be granted the liberty to do things because they are inherently worth doing. One engages in work because it is meaningful, and if it is not, one changes the work.... This revisioned life feels better in the end, for such a person experiences his or her life as rich with meaning, and opening to a larger and larger mystery (154).

Your interest in this book may be stimulated by a desire to understand, reconcile, or assess your life and/or career(s) to date. Your motivation may be to evaluate options or choices in your immediate or longer-term future. You may wish to deepen or enhance your present experience. Perhaps, as a result of this guided exploration, you will discover a career overflowing with riches that you wish to sustain or transplant into new endeavors. Perhaps you will identify disappointments, unfulfilled desires, or lost ambitions; or perhaps you will discover unanticipated benefits derived from a less-demanding career track. Maybe you will choose to stay the course, launch dramatic changes, or make small adjustments. Maybe you will discover a deep satisfaction and contentment with your life and work and discover that that inspires others.

Regardless of the outcome, engaging with this book positions you to enter into the last stage of a career consciously and deliberately. This is your opportunity, from the advantage of experience, to create a satisfying and enriching transition and new season. As such, I encourage you to enter into this process without any notion of "shoulds," problems that must be fixed, or issues that demand to be resolved. This is not about correcting anything that is wrong or bad or broken, it is about creating what you desire.

At any stage or season of life, you can harvest your experience and sort the bounty in order to evaluate what has reached fruition and what you yet wish to cultivate for yourself or others. You may harvest to reap your yield and to yield with grace and blessings to those who are growing around you.

You may wish to pause and consider whether you hope to discover something in particular or if you are beginning this journey simply with wonder. What emotions are aroused in you at the prospective of embarking on this journey? What outcomes will indicate to you that the sojourn has been fulfilling? What intentions or purposes are known to you at this point?

envisioning *Using metaphors to harvest*

What happens when I make a metaphorical connection? I gain a creative perspective by looking at things differently…. A surge of energy loosens rigid assumptions, opening up new possibilities and deepening my understanding.
Rosalie Deer Heart and Alison Strickland (94)

Shakespeare, Homer, Dante, Chaucer, saw the splendor of meaning that plays over the visible world; knew that a tree had another use than for apples, and corn another than for meal, and the ball of the earth, than for tillage and roads: that these things bore a second and finer harvest to the mind, being emblems of its thoughts, and conveying in all their natural history a certain mute commentary on human life.
Ralph Waldo Emerson

Metaphor consists of images connected to something they literally cannot be. Metaphors create tension and excitement by producing new connections, and in doing so reveal a truth about the world we had not previously recognized…. [T]hat is the power of metaphor, to surprise us, make us catch our breath, illuminate an aspect of the world that is totally at odds with the conventional way of seeing it.
Gabriele Lusser Rico (187, 189)

The right cerebral hemisphere in most people is the residence of the metaphoric mind. This is the 'left-handed' domain. When an idea comes into the metaphoric mind, a sudden rush of relationships flashes into being and the original thought expands rapidly outward into a network of new holistic perceptions. The role of metaphoric thinking is to invent, to create, and to challenge conformity by extending what is known into new meadows of knowing. The metaphoric mind treats all input as fragments of reality, and as soon as a fragment appears, the mind begins the search for the whole. Like an archeologist who discovers a tiny fragment of an ancient pot, the metaphoric mind at once begins to visualize the whole creation. ***Bob Samples*** (14)

We commonly use metaphors to understand and explain concepts. By comparing a concept or object that is new or unfamiliar with something that is known and understood, we also give meaning to the new. It's wonderful to me how even a commonplace image or action used as a metaphor can trigger a fresh comparison rich in illuminating similarities.

I have long used metaphors as teaching and learning tools in workshops. When doing so, I explain that a metaphor is an abstract parallel representation or "a figure of speech in which a term or phrase is applied to something to which it is not literally applicable in order to suggest a resemblance." [metaphor. Dictionary.com. Dictionary.com Unabridged (v 1.1). Random House, Inc. http://dictionary. reference.com/browse/metaphor (accessed: July 04, 2007).] I also share that the word metaphor is derived from the Greek prefix *meta*, meaning "over or across" and *pherein*, meaning "to carry or bear." The Greek word *metaphora* means a "transfer" or "carrying over," as in the case of one word to another. [metaphor. Dictionary.com. Online Etymology Dictionary. Douglas Harper, Historian. http://dictionary.reference.com/browse/ metaphor (accessed: May 13, 2008).] To harvest the bounty of your career in subsequent chapters, you will consider the nature and meaning of trees and carry over that meaning to your career. For example, you will look at how the roots of a tree function as its foundation and then explore the foundation or roots of your career. You will consider the branches of a tree as a metaphor for how you have extended yourself professionally through relationships. And, you will transfer the meaning of fruit to the value of professional accomplishments or legacies in your life.

When we use a metaphor to explore a personal concern, we can relate to aspects of the concern as if they were outside of our self. We can thus position ourselves in a safe distance of "one-step removed" while exploring the representation of the issue more deeply because we are somewhat detached and because the metaphoric substitution exposes the issue in a fresh light. Along with detachment and distance from the topic, a metaphor also provides full-sensory engagement, which offers an enriching, creative context for problem solving. Metaphor engages both the left and right brain and stimulates interaction between them.

My husband likes to say that metaphor can obfuscate when we need to *talk* straight, but metaphor clarifies when we need to *think* straight.

envisioning *The tree as metaphor*

When a massive oak tree or a giant redwood reaches maturity, it offers shelter and support for creatures too numerable to mention. Yet, having reached its maximum strength, it has also become more vulnerable. It offers protection against the wind, but now its size and weight make it more susceptible to damage from storms. The essence we perceive as we look upon the majesty of the great tree is vitality. Its vitality keeps it standing, storm after storm. Vitality characterizes maturity in having a response to the forces that stand in the way of the tree's existence. ***Charles D. Hayes*** (136)

Among archetypal images, the Sacred Tree is one of the most widely known symbols on Earth. There are few cultures in which the Sacred Tree does not figure: as an image of the cosmos, as a dwelling place of gods or spirits, as a medium of prophecy and knowledge, and as an agent of metamorphoses when the tree is transformed into human or divine form or when it bears a divine or human image as its fruit or flowers. ***Christopher and Tricia McDowell***

Tree, gather up my thoughts
like the clouds in your branches.
Draw up my soul
like the waters in your root.
In the arteries of your trunk
bring me together.
Through your leaves
breathe out the sky.
J. Daniel Beaudry, *"Breath"*

Stand Tall and Proud
Sink your roots deeply into the Earth
Reflect the light of a greater source
Think long term
Go out on a limb
Remember your place among all living beings
Embrace with joy the changing seasons
For each yields its own abundance
The Energy and Birth of Spring
The Growth and Contentment of Summer
The Wisdom to let go of leaves in the Fall
The Rest and Quiet Renewal of Winter
Ilan Shamir, *"Advice From a Tree"*

What did the tree learn from the earth
to be able to talk with the sky? ***Pablo Neruda***

Trees are poems that earth writes upon the sky.
Kahlil Gibran

A Tree of Life, Tree of Knowledge, Tree of Speech, or World Tree occupies a central position in many cultural and religious stories and myths. A tree can be an ideal setting for true love or for enlightenment. Genealogy is often presented in the form of a family tree. A tree is also an apt metaphor for a career. Consider all that trees provide humanity and the planet: food, medicine, shelter, fuel, wildlife habitat, wilderness, climate, oxygen, landscaping, inspiration, and places to climb, build "houses," or suspend swings. Trees provide wood—perhaps the planet's most versatile and beautiful building and crafting material. Trees are a wellspring of creative sustenance and enrichment for all life.

Consider all that a career may have provided you: income, health care and other benefits, daily and annual structure, physical and/or virtual space to do your work, goals and objectives, lifestyle, connections, relationships, role, position, identity, status, purpose, challenges, outlet for skills and abilities, personal and professional development, social life, transportation choices, service and other opportunities to contribute to something larger than yourself, perhaps something socially beneficial. Often our career determines where and how we live, with whom we socialize and form relationships, if and when we have children, where our children go to school, with whom they interact, opportunities to travel for business and/or pleasure, how we travel, how we transport ourselves and our family, how we are of service to others and our community, and when and how we retire.

Whether what you have received or experienced as a result of a career has proven beneficial or unsatisfactory, promoted or restrained your growth, or been what you always desired or ultimately dreaded, it is likely that your life was formed and shaped to a great extent by your career, and that your career provided you with roots, branches, fruits, and seeds.

As Jacqueline Paterson points out in *Tree Wisdom*, there is great "affinity possible between trees and people...we are closely akin to them, following the same cycles throughout our lives' span. For they, like us, stand upright, their 'feet' in (or on) the earth and their 'bodies' and 'heads' in the air" (5). In fact, trees share many characteristics with humanity. They reproduce sexually, and develop through seasons and stages with a protracted maturation and long life. Descriptors of tree physiology parallel human anatomy—trunk or torso, limbs, crown, crotch, cells, veins, circulation, respiration, and even memory, as growth rings stored in the cortex and as markers of natural and human events. Trees even project moods through a changing appearance as the seasons shift.

Every tree is unique and a product of both genes (nature) and environment (nurture). They grow where planted, but are more likely to thrive in a healthy environment. Their relationship with other life forms and the environment is symbiotic—requiring appropriate sunlight, water, and nourishment. Trees are integral to the quality of air, soil, climate, and weather; they also provide protection, shelter and nourishment for wildlife sharing their environs. Trees evolve, and yet the form of the tree sapling remains forever imbedded in the growing trunk, retaining the essence of its youth and offering the core upon which growth develops. Trees grow tougher, wider, and deeper with age.

Despite being anchored to one place, the lives of trees are long and changing. Trees are deeply connected to the earth and are always reaching for the sky. They are in concert with the elements and the planets. Trees have always suggested spiritual connections and significance. They are often experienced as sentient, and may impart information, knowledge, and even wisdom to those who seek it. They create inviting and inspiring places, inspire meaning and metaphor, and manifest beauty. Who can fail to appreciate the value and majesty of trees?

You can bring your own life to this tree metaphor by beginning to experience it imaginatively. In subsequent chapters you will be guided to imaginatively experience roots, branches, fruits, and seeds. Right now, you can experience your self as an entire tree.

experience yourself as a tree imaginatively

Just for a moment, imagine that you are a tree—perhaps an oak, a pine, or the apple tree you used to climb as a child. Start by imagining your tree self in a forest, garden, or the setting of your choice. Choose a time of year, a time of day, and other details that will support your imaginative experience. How tall is your tree self? What is the texture of your bark? What color are your leaves or needles? What is your overall shape? Are you bearing fruit or sheltering nests? What else comes to mind for you?

Now, imagine your core essence rising from the warm, moist, nourishing soil, expanding first downwards, then upwards, your crown reaching towards the life-giving sun.

Imagine, beneath the soil, securing you firmly, a vast network of branching roots, gradually narrowing from their widest circumference just at and below the soil to countless minute strands that spread out underground from your root tips to suck nourishing water and minerals from the warm, moist soil. As you extend and expand upwards, ever approaching the source of light, so you extend and expand downwards into the generative soil, which you in turn enrich, renew, and protect from dispersal.

Feel how your core supports a framework of branches that narrow as they reach outwards and upwards, holding your leaves or needles up to receive the sun's light, warmth and nourishment. Feel your tree self give birth to buds and grow thicker and sturdier to support more branches, more buds, more leaves, and fruit. Envision yourself growing taller as new branches emerge above the trunk at your crown to maximize your leaves' exposure to the sun's energy.

Appreciate the beauty of your flowers or cones, the reproductive structures that generate, allow fertilization of, and protect your seeds. Feel the magic of your seeds. Each one is a culmination and a new beginning; each one is pure essence and raw potential; each one is what remains and then what continues… With the growth of flowers, fruit, and seeds, your life cycle comes full circle, and with the germination and growth of each seed, a new life cycle begins.

Imagine yourself as a tree in each season. After a long and deep wintry dreaming, you become dimly aware of increased light and warmth. Gradually you feel your surroundings and your own insides beginning to rouse, a resurgence of sap moving, flowing. Your awareness of new growth is like a subtle yearning, stretching, reaching. A celebration begins to stir, and soon life, growth, deepening warmth and refreshing moisture permeate your being.

Eventually, change is signaled by the angle and quality of the light. As if in celebration of the busy harvest and the restful season to come, you adorn yourself in brilliant finery. Then, a gradual lessening gives way to preparing—leaves scattered, seeds released, sap slowed, buds stabilized, bark hardened.

Now you stand proudly against the stark sky, your form revealed, your essence exposed. You embody the darkness of the gathering season, the lowering clouds. Your exposed roots assume the shapes of reptiles dreaming in anticipation. Your falling leaves cascade into a secret dance or tumble and leap in a drunken revel. Your branches grasp at weakening rays, gasp at bitter winds. A proud new silhouette appears, imperious presence reclaimed. You have shed all pretense to manifest endurance, to liberate your crone. And, you are one—with your self, the season, and the earth.

And, now… gradually resume your human form and consciousness.

Alan Watts once said that "…the growing seed is gathering nourishment from its environment, but the process is no mere sticking together of the nutritive elements, for it absorbs and transforms them…" (Samples, 51). I hope that the culmination of your experiences within this book will not only prove transformative, but also expand your options for and satisfaction in propagating the fulfillment of the next cycle of your life.

Acorns

Having read this chapter, what particularly stimulates or energizes you?

What holds the most value for you?

What deliberate process(es) are you inspired to create?

What spontaneous process(es) do you expect you will have the opportunity to allow?

If you underlined, doodled, or journaled as you read this chapter, review that now and notice:

Any meaning evident now that was not apparent as you wrote or drew.

Anything that surprises or particularly pleases you.

Any redundancies or patterns.

Anything you wish to complete or follow up with.

How might you compare your career and/or your self to a tree?

Ask yourself:

What are some of my favorite memories of my career?

What have I invested of myself in my career?

How many different ways can I depict the culmination of my career?

What nourishment for others and myself can the gifts of my career still provide?

Go through this chapter again and respond to the in-text questions. Notice anywhere you feel uncertain, incomplete, intrigued, or pulled, which may provide important clues about how you have yet to fulfill your career…

How do you wish to benefit from this chapter?

Return to this exercise at intervals during your Harvesting process and beyond to notice any changes in your responses.

Stepping Stones

To harvest your career is to gather for review your experiences of working life, take stock of the resultant inner bounty, and consider a cornucopia of choices for creating a conscious, relevant, and personally satisfying next season of life.

Narrative Journaling

Return to page 28 and reread the first three paragraphs. Respond to them now in your journal.

Visual Journaling

Visually represent the yield of your career as some colorful abstraction. Remember to be relaxed and playful. The point is to access the creative part of your brain; and scribbles or doodles will do that quite effectively, especially if you use colors and just have fun.

On another page, allow aspects of the first abstraction to become something different. Fill as many pages with colorful developments as you wish. Consider the *process* of allowing one thing to become something different.

Interpersonal Experiences

Ask several retired individuals how they continue to reap the yield of their career.

Workplace Applications

Ask several colleagues if they have considered sprouting a new endeavor from the experiences of their career.

origins and underpinnings,
groundedness and stability, regulation
and survival...

roots

anchoring What has supported you as a professional?
nourishing What fosters your growth?

Your past is not your potential. In any hour you can choose to liberate the future.
Marilyn Ferguson

A little too abstract, a little too wise,
It is time for us to kiss the earth again,
It is time to let the leaves rain from the skies,
Let the rich life run to the roots again.
Robinson Jeffers

…whatever good or bad fortune may come our way we can always give it meaning and transform it into something of value.
Hermann Hesse

It's a good lesson to return to our roots after a period of activity to offer gratitude for the blossoming and go within for a time, honoring the alternating rhythms of nature that empower our lives as we cultivate the gardens within and around us. *Diane Dreher* (45)

Not that the past can be changed, but by altering our perspective on it we might then be able to create our future. *Erin Sullivan* (89)

The past is not your potential for potential has no bounds. Choose to break free from your self-imposed limits. Use your imagination to create a life of endless possibility. Experience your magnificence first hand. *Frankie Picasso*

You need to claim the events of your life to make yourself yours. When you truly possess all you have been and done, which may take some time, you are fierce with reality.
Florida Scott-Maxwell

If I were to wish for anything, I should not wish for wealth and power, but for the passionate sense of the potential… what wine is so sparkling, so fragrant, so intoxicating, as possibility! *Søren Kierkegaard*

43

In this chapter and the next three, we will use the metaphor of a tree to consider your career. Is your career employment from which you have recently retired or a position from which you will soon retire? Is your career a life-long profession or a variety of roles and circumstances? Whatever your answers, the tree metaphor gives you the opportunity to explore your career, however you define it, in terms of the roots or foundation, branches or relationships, fruits or accomplishments, and seeds or culmination and new beginning. Let's begin with your "roots."

Roots, of course, begin with a seed. When a seed sprouts, the first growth to emerge is the root. From the primary root or taproot, smaller branch or lateral roots grow and form a continuously expanding system or network. These roots permeate the earth to locate water and minerals. They also store food as they extend deeper into the ground to collect more nutrients for the growing sapling and eventually for a developed trunk, branches, leaves, and perhaps flowers and fruit.

When I walk past mature trees and notice exposed roots, what seem to be gnarled, earth-born branches suggest slumbering reptiles, secretly breathing a life force and soon to awaken and stretch. Since that may not be a pleasing picture to you, try allowing your own image to form as you walk past trees and observe their visible roots. Imagine you are seeing a tree for the first time. What might you wonder about those earth-bound forms that are only partially exposed? Or, can you imagine sinking your bare feet into the earth to touch the unseen, moist, warm roots of your favorite tree? Perhaps you'd rather imagine that your own legs are roots extending deep within the earth.

Among your own observations, try asking yourself some of the following questions: What do roots suggest to your mind? What do you notice about them? Are you able to connect with them? Do you notice any similarities between them and your self? If you were a tree, what would your root system look like? Feel like? What kind of conversation would you have with them? Recall the image that came to your mind when you imaginatively experienced your self as a tree in the "To Harvest" chapter. How would you expand your previous vision of roots to include these new insights and images?

You may also wish to place plant cuttings in a clear container of water to observe the roots germinate and grow. Imagine those same fragile white strands making their way through the dark soil. Using all six of your senses, allow yourself to imagine what that might look, feel, taste, smell, sound, and be like.

The roots of a plant or a tree are its foundation. Although the bulk of the roots lies beneath the ground, they are that from which the entire tree arose; and they remain that which nourishes and sustains. Roots provide security and support, both holding a tree firm and allowing it to grow. Just as a tree's roots give rise to its growth and development, your past enables your present and provides for possibility and new growth in the future. In this way, your background, history, experiences, and memories are all examples of your roots.

Metaphorically, roots suggest origins and underpinnings, groundedness and stability, regulation and survival. What other associations to the concept of roots come to your mind?

An individual described as deeply rooted may be set in her ways and resistant to change. Or, she may feel supported and secure and thus comfortable with growth and change. If you describe someone as rootless, are you implying that she embraces change and adventure or that she seeks to escape her past and avoid commitment? Did your early family life provide deep roots for a fulfilling adulthood, or have you cultivated and propagated your own root system in order to thrive? Where would you place yourself on a "rootedness" spectrum?

Tree roots are pathways for new growth. Although new growth causes old parts of the root system to die off, the residue continues to serve by conditioning the soil. The traces of former pathways also leave a record of development. How do you trace your development? What pathways in your life seem to have been most significant in forming you—family, places of residence, schools, friends, talents, interests, jobs, careers?

The root and branch systems of a tree are reflective of one another. The girth and height of a tree are determined by the health and extent of its roots, and the overall health of the tree results from the health of its roots. Without a vibrant root system, a tree will never reach its potential. Conversely, a tree that develops beyond the capacity of its roots will be always be threatened by the elements. If you ever feel "rootless," consider the stretch of your branches and the nourishment that your life has created for you to thrive. If you ever feel that you are not "fulfilling your potential," consider the extent of your roots and your capacity to realize your desires.

experience roots imaginatively

Imagine dark, embracing, moist warmth—only that. Imagine, aware and observant only through sensation and motion, a gliding, gliding slowly into a caressing deepness, seeking nourishment from the wisdom of the soil, the earth as source of life. Imagine roots beneath the soil—reaching and growing downward and outward to suck nourishing water and minerals from the warm, moist, generative soil.

Imagine roots as a vast network of branches, gradually narrowing from their widest circumference just at and below the soil to countless minute strands that spread out underground. As branches extend and expand upward to the life-giving sun, so roots extend and expand downward into the generative soil, which they in turn enrich, renew, and protect from dispersal.

Experience roots, deep and abiding, as life source—essential and vital, supporting and strengthening a tree, enabling it to grow. Feel the strength of your roots as they sustain what has been and feed what is emerging. Acknowledge your roots as pathways to your growth, development, and new direction. Witness how, like the trunk, they preserve a record of your development, leaving traces of the pathways that have enabled your growth.

Your "You" arises from your roots. How have you/do you change as your nourishment varies? What forms of nourishment have your environments or circumstances provided and what forms have you deliberately sought out, cultivated, provided for yourself? What has nourished you, what does nourish you, and what would you like to take nourishment from? Is there some new endeavor, relationship, service, lifestyle, setting, form of self-expression, or creative activity that is calling to you?

As you consider your roots, notice your patterns and growth tracks. Notice how your roots enable your present and future and provide for possibility.

anchoring *What has supported you as a professional?*

As you consider the botanical function of a tree's root system and the metaphorical applications of roots to your career, allow yourself to breath slowly and deeply for a moment. On an exhale, begin to contemplate the question: *What has supported me as a professional?* Does a ready answer come to mind for you or do you foresee yourself choosing to engage in a deeper exploration of your professional root system?

Try viewing your life as a continuum so as to identify foundational interests, talents, accomplishments, skills, and desires that have woven themselves through your experiences and choices. Look for patterns and growth tracks. Can you see traits and inclinations that arose during your childhood and have manifested in your adult activities? I remember, for example, that early in my elementary years I wrote that I wanted to be a teacher and an artist. I never became either of those aspirations per se, but, as a librarian, I have consistently created opportunities to teach, apply my creativity, and be involved with art—teaching research skills and a variety of workshops, promoting my library, and coordinating exhibits and art shows. My child self was certainly mother to my professional woman!

Review your different jobs or positions—perhaps as listed on your resume. How did each arise, conclude, and lead to the next? Which choices were driven by desire and which by needs or "shoulds"? Did you ever take time out or work part time? Were there any possibilities you now consider lost opportunities? Did some jobs prove more useful than expected? Did you experience any obstacles to advancement? In retrospect, do you think any obstacles were imposed by outer circumstance or by your self? What kinds of differences did it make being a woman professional? How did you blend working with your personal life, family, etc.? What did you give up to be a professional woman? What did you gain? Would you make any changes? How would you characterize your career "path"?

If a crystal ball had displayed your career to yourself as a teen, would you have been surprised? Disappointed? Pleased? If you could visit your teen self as you are now and reveal what would come, how would you present it? How do you think your teen self would respond?

Consider the quality of your work day-to-days. Focus for a moment on days that are particularly stimulating, enjoyable, and satisfying—days when you feel you are doing what you like and do best. What characterizes such days? Do you recall particular activities, interactions, or accomplishments? Did the stimulation come from what you were doing, who you were doing it with, or the end results? Are such days memorable because you initiated an activity, made significant progress, or reached closure?

What are your ideal working conditions? Do you prefer solitude or interaction? Are you more relationship or task oriented? Do you seek direction and structure or autonomy and flexibility? Do you thrive on consistency or variety? Are you more steadfast or innovative? Are you more comfortable in a leadership, collaborative, or supportive role? What are your environmental preferences? How will you integrate your preferences into your next stage?

What has kept you going when you've felt overwhelmed or exhausted? How have you learned to release and relieve stress? What has motivated or energized you? When have you felt deep connections to your profession or workplace? Do friends or family provide an important support system? What kinds of support will you create for the current transition and beyond?

In the survey of 6,000 preretirees by Steven Shagrin, from *Facts about Retiring in the United States* [no other information provided in cite by Newman in *Retiring as a Career*, p.32], respondents indicated the following as what attracted them to their work:

Feeling challenged by my work.

Liking the people I work with.

Having the opportunity to learn.

Traveling for the company.

Working as a team member.

Helping the company grow.

Being part of a respected company.

Receiving the income and benefits.

Influencing the company's direction and success.

To what extent do you resonate with this list? What would you add or eliminate?

How has your position, career, or profession nourished your life roots? Is there anything remaining for you to do within your career to strengthen your own personal roots?

You are being prompted to consider a lot of questions! Do you feel like a metaphorical tree in a heavy rain? Is that sensation unpleasant or energizing? Either way, pause for another deep breath. Allow the impact of all these questions and considerations to soften and be absorbed. Know that your inner being will continue to process your responses, in both mind and heart, and that you can just relax into the expansion that will result. You may wish now to simply continue breathing or to jot down a paragraph or list of what has supported you as a professional. You may wish to resume the mantle of your tree self to consider what has supported your professional growth.

When I consider what has supported me as a professional, I recognize that in 30 years of being an academic librarian I certainly have had moments in which I wished to be released from the constraints and stresses of a career. Any thoughts of leaving my job, academia, or the profession, however, have always served to clarify what keeps me in the same place—like a vibrant root system. I value being a part of something that has clear social value. More often than not, I find my work engaging and stimulating. I thrive on the variety and flexibility my job provides. I also have a strong desire to accomplish and to contribute to the responsiveness and sustained growth of a service that must meet changing needs. I enjoy positive, mutually supportive social interaction—even that which is apparently superficial, but nevertheless authentic.

I have always loved learning. I have deliberately developed a variety of skills that I enjoy using to support learning, such as "mind mapping" (as featured by Tony Buzan in The Mind Map Book), as well as various accelerated learning and PhotoReading (www.photoreading.com) techniques. I appreciate that my work challenges me to pursue new learning and to continuously apply my skills to do so.

One of my colleagues, in contrast, is supported as a professional by consistent routines and expectations. She likes knowing what to expect each day and the satisfaction of accomplishing what she set out to do. She is goal-oriented and works steadily towards goals. She feels supported when her punctuality and reliability are appreciated. Task-oriented, she is not comfortable when committee meetings devolve into socializing. She does not protest or complain when change is required, but adapts methodically. She takes in new information and develops new skills independently. After taking time to process and integrate, she may create documents and procedures that support others.

nourishing What fosters your growth?

Evolution always transcends and includes, incorporates and goes beyond. **Ken Wilber**

To be creative means to consider the whole process of life as a process of birth, and not to take any stage of life as a final stage. Most people die before they are fully born. Creativeness means to be born before one dies. **Erich Fromm**

Reality is the conversation between ourselves and the never-ending productions of time. The closer we get to the source of the productions of time—that is, to the eternal—the more easily we understand the particular currents we must navigate on any given day. **David Whyte** (180)

Allow yourself again to breath slowly and deeply for a moment. On an inhale, consider the question: *What fosters my growth?* Does a ready answer come to mind for you or will you choose to engage in a deeper exploration of this theme?

In the imaginative experience above, you considered the various forms of nourishment that life has provided you and that you have cultivated for yourself. Of course, in addition to basic sources of nourishment required to grow, we must also seek nutriments to sustain our development. As you continue to imagine the roots of a tree branching out and stretching in order to grow and support the growth of the tree, relax into this next series of questions that will support your growth.

What prompted you to become a professional or enter your field? How did you gain the skills and knowledge necessary to begin your career? How have you kept up-to-date and maintained your professional expertise? How have you prepared yourself for new responsibilities, advancement, or promotions? What stands out for you as developmental markers? Identify the similarities and differences between your professional and personal development efforts. As you create your next season of life, are you considering how you will continue to foster growth and development?

Consider what has supported you in your professional growth and development. Have you had supervisors, mentors, or colleagues who have recognized and encouraged your strengths? Have you structured your own continuous professional development or benefited from occasional boosts to your skills or knowledge? Have you risen to challenges posed by new responsibilities or positions? Do you participate in professional activities or organizations, publish or present?

What developmental advances in your life and career have you deliberately moved towards? What motivated you? How did you sustain your determination? How did you generate patience and learn to trust the process? How did you know when the transition was complete? Did you celebrate your achievement? In retrospect, your previous growth processes can reveal patterns to illuminate your present and empower you to more deliberately create the future.

What has fostered the growth and development of your workplace and profession? In what ways have you contributed to the growth and development of your workplace and profession?

As I consider what fosters my growth, I know that autonomy, flexibility, creativity, and self-expression are vital. Although I have not sought advancement or promotion in terms of a career ladder, fresh endeavors are important to me. Graced with a fundamentally humane workplace where professional development is valued, I have been able to create opportunities for new challenges, growth, and change by redirecting my responsibilities and priorities over the years. This has been critical for me given 28 years in the same library with only two different, and lateral, positions.

Many outstanding professional models in my own field as well as others have inspired me to expand as a professional. I am also motivated by opportunities to share information, knowledge, and cultural resources with others.

I have noticed other patterns of growth among friends. One of my colleagues always seems to be up on the latest professional literature. She frequently reviews books in the field for professional journals. She is often an early adopter of new technologies. Professional development is usually a solo activity for her, and she rarely attends workshops or conferences. In contrast, one of my friends has always been a rising star. Outgoing and articulate, she is a natural networker and seems to know everyone in her field. She loves to learn in group settings, and attends many conferences and professional development workshops annually. Many mentors have fostered her growth, as she constantly takes on new challenges in her upwardly mobile career.

Clarity about what has supported you as professional over the years and what fosters your growth is a first step in determining how you will transition to a new season. Your traits and experiences will continue to ground you as you move forward and to sustain you as you encounter new choices and experiences. You could even imagine that as a fresh, new professional you were just an acorn. Now, as you look to a new season, you are a magnificent, tall oak—still anchored and nourished by the roots that gave rise to you and continue to nourish you.

Acorns

Having read this chapter, what particularly stimulates or energizes you?

What holds the most value for you?

What deliberate process(es) are you inspired to create?

What spontaneous process(es) do you expect you will have the opportunity to allow?

If you underlined, doodled, or journaled as you read this chapter, review that now and notice:

Any meaning evident now that was not apparent as you wrote or drew.

Anything that surprises or particularly pleases you.

Any redundancies or patterns.

Anything you wish to complete or follow up with.

Go through this chapter again and respond to the in-text questions. Notice anywhere you feel uncertain, incomplete, intrigued, or pulled, which may provide important clues about how you have yet to fulfill your career…

Ask yourself:

What roots have I grown as a result of my career?

What roots have I contributed to my workplace?

In what ways has my career provided a root system for my life?

What nourishes my roots and all that arises from them?

What will I take from my roots and cultivate in the next arc of my life spiral? Your answer to this question may suggest an element of the future you are now creating.

How do you wish to benefit from this chapter?

Return to these questions at intervals during your Harvesting process and beyond to notice any changes in your responses.

Stepping Stones

The purpose of exploring roots is to identify the environmental conditions, sources of nourishment, and growth patterns that have brought you to this season of life. Giving rise to and sustaining you from beneath the surface, your roots are your origins, what grounds you, and what regulates your life. Your roots enable your future.

Narrative Journaling

Review of the past can offer inspiration for new directions. What "time markers" of your life are available to you? Have you kept journals, photo albums, and/or mementos? Have you maintained school, employment, or health records? How about records of pets? How do you mark birthdays, anniversaries, and other special occasions? Do you distribute a family "newsletter"? Do you have a central place to record major family events, such as births, marriages, deaths? What other approaches have you used as record keeping in your life?

Consider as well your professional records—have you maintained a resume or vita? Recorded major personnel events, such as promotions and raises? Listed employment anniversaries or achievements? Written annual reports or evaluations? You may even find your tax reports and other financial documents informative. What other approaches have you used as record keeping in your career? You might also consider your role in preserving your workplace memory.

Once you have determined what is already available to you, consider what would be useful to you now and how you might go about collecting or compiling that information. Approaches to a career or life review can be conventional or creative, i.e., nonlinear, thematic, or non-narrative. Perhaps you would like to write a narrative autobiography covering your entire life or focusing on your career, intellectual/spiritual development, or some other aspect of your life especially important to you. You may find it easier to create a timeline or other type of graph. Perhaps you would prefer to ask someone else to take your "oral history" or speak into a recorder for transcribing later. The task will feel manageable if you chunk it down—addressing seven or ten-year periods, for example, or pre-school, elementary, high school, college, first job, subsequent employment, etc. Another approach is to cover themes over time, such as key relationships, education, employment, residences, etc. Or, be more playful—write up your own "best" and "worst" lists, your most embarrassing moments, your most inspired moments, your fifteen minutes of fame.

You may further wish to review and reflect upon your career and life by engaging with some of the following activities.

Review and reflect on your career
Respond to the following questions without preliminary reflection:
What did I bring to my career? What did I give? What did I receive?

Consider the root system of your workplace—what anchors and nourishes it—including its history, mission, goals, values, accomplishments, personnel, clients/customers. In what ways have you contributed to the current state of your workplace? In what ways are your contributions part of the root system that sustains your workplace, keeping it healthy and growing? Are there any contributions you would yet like to make to your workplace that would nourish and strengthen its roots?

If you were to visually represent the roots of your career, what would they look like—size, shape/form, color, texture? How would they be presented? Are they shallow and wide ranging or deep and penetrating or both?

Write about the wisdom you have gained from your work. What lessons have you learned? How will you go about applying your wisdom in the future?

In what ways has your career provided a root system for your life—e.g., financially, daily/yearly routines/structure, professional and social contacts, achievements and acknowledgements…?

Having completed your career review, look for themes, patterns, unfinished business, questions, regrets, lessons, high points, inspiration, hopes, plans…

Review and reflect on your life

Write your autobiography or compile it from journals and/or other self-records.

Write your biography from the perspective of another (e.g., a parent or child, friend or co-worker, acquaintance or stranger observing you, etc.).

Write an essay about highlights of your life or the meaning of your life.

Write a short story (or even a novel!) about yourself.

Write your eulogy or obituary.

Write a letter about yourself, introducing yourself to someone unknown.

Write an introduction of yourself as if you were to be a speaker or presenter.

Interview yourself for a magazine or newspaper article, or ask someone else to do so (submit it?!).

If you were to visually represent the roots of your life, what would they look like—size, shape/form, color, texture? How would they be presented? Are they shallow and wide ranging or deep and penetrating or both?

What questions do you have for your roots? What answers do they provide? What do you require from them to thrive?   What questions do your roots have for you?

What nourishes your roots and therefore all that arises from them—family, friends, lovers, community, service, church, spirituality, nature, vocation, avocation, location?

Do you ever feel "root bound"? If so, how will you open more space for yourself?

Conversely, do you ever feel that your roots are too shallow or insufficient? If so, how will you nourish and develop them?

Having completed your life review, look for themes, patterns, unfinished business, questions, regrets, lessons, high points, inspiration, hopes, plans…

Visual Journaling

Create a realistic or abstract representation of roots, and let it speak to you. What questions does it pose? What answers does it suggest? What does it need or want? How does it communicate?

Visually represent the roots of your career and/or life as you described above or instead of describing them verbally.

Rapidly sketch a depiction of roots underground. Write, on the branches of the roots, qualities, experiences, or activities that ground, nourish, and sustain you.

Create a collage of roots. Contemplate your collage in the next day or two. What does it suggest? What stands out? What is missing? Is there anything you would like to change? What is particularly grounding for you?

Having completed your visual journaling for this section, look for themes, patterns, unfinished business, questions, regrets, lessons, high points, inspiration, hopes, plans…

Interpersonal Experiences

Share with someone the steps that brought each of you to your current positions. How intentional or happenstance were they? In retrospect, did the outcome serve you well, or would you prefer to recreate the path?

Ask a relative or someone who has known you all or most of your life to describe your development and your attributes.

Ask someone to write you a recommendation for the next stage of your life.

Workplace Applications

What comprises the institutional memory of your workplace? Evaluate its usefulness and suggest improvements.

Develop a process for gathering oral histories from those who retire from your workplace.

Collect oral histories from and honor already retired colleagues who were with the organization for a significant period of time.

branches

extending How did you develop your most satisfying working relationships and professional connections?

shaping How do you strengthen and diversify your relationships and connections?

Have you ever noticed a tree
standing naked against the sky,
How beautiful it is?
All its branches are outlined,
and in its nakedness
There is a poem, there is a song.
Krishnamurti

Knowledge is not achieved until shared.
Unknown

Knowledge speaks but wisdom listens.
Unknown

Wisdom is the reward you get for a lifetime of
listening when you would have preferred to talk.
Doug Larson

Wishing to be friends is quick work, but
friendship is a slow-ripening fruit. *Aristotle*

...friendship...is essential to intellectuals. You
can date the evolving life of a mind, like the age
of a tree, by the rings of friendship formed by
the expanding central trunk. *Mary McCarthy*

Building and maintaining networks across
generations, organizations, and cultures is a way
to learn continuously and to leverage the insights
of people who have a genuine interest in your
growth and success.
Warren Bennis and Robert Thomas

Let's continue to develop the tree metaphor with an exploration of branches—the branches that give shape and form to a tree, and the relationships that give shape and form to personal and professional endeavors. Recall for a moment, your imaginative experience of a tree and its branches in the "To Harvest" chapter. Try stretching out your arms and fingers, imagining they are branches—opening, summoning, holding. Allow your spine to lengthen and feel the crown of your head as if it is the crown of a tree. If you were a tree, how would the branches along the length of your trunk reflect the changing seasons?

I grew up in California and now live in Colorado, where I have the pleasure of experiencing four distinct seasons. Following the transformative autumn, the weather may ease us into winter, but by late January the Boulder valley landscape presents a limited palette, and the steadfast pines seem to be the last remaining plant life on our bit of earth. Because of this period of muted dormancy, I grow giddy with the renewal of plant diversity in spring. One of my springtime pleasures is observing the slow awakening of trees and the extraordinary variety among their buds and processes of unfolding. Even in California, of course, the season brings new growth and new bursts of color.

Wherever you live, what do you notice about trees as they awaken in the spring? Try observing how buds vary in size, shape, color, positioning on the branch, and relationship to each other. If you look closely, you can observe that some buds produce flowers while others open to reveal a miniature leaf. Similarly, some flowers may precede leaves, or blossoms and leaves may decorate a tree simultaneously.

While witnessing this daily transformation, I experience the rebirth as if it were occurring in slow motion. And then one morning it is as if it was all completed quite suddenly, and tree branches, which so recently appeared as drab, forlorn clusters of sticks, are adorned in glorious greens to dance with the breezes and birds. And, I notice how the space around familiar trees is altered from the previous spring by boughs extended and fulfilled.

I have learned only recently that it is no less satisfying to observe the branches of trees in the winter when leaves have given way to reveal the foundational architecture of deciduous trees. Try noticing for yourself differences in how branches align with the trunk, ground, and each other. Take note of distinctions in girth, length, shape, and quantity of branches. You can also see how bark colors vary widely not only among different species of trees, but also within the same specie depending on the age of the tree and the effects of light and shade. You can also notice variations in bark on a single tree, from the rough and textured trunk to the smoother and more vibrantly colored limbs and branches.

Shadows of leafless trees, whether produced by sunlight or a full moon, reveal much about the varieties of tree architecture. I especially enjoy looking up at patterns of branches highlighted against the changing colors of the sky by day or night.

Whatever the season, notice how branches radiate outward to receive light, nutrients, and moisture. In this way, branches not only result from but also mirror the roots. Notice how they provide the overall symmetry to a tree, and yet individual branches are irregular and diverse. Think about how branches both reflect and define the season. Imagine looking at a tree from the perspective of a bird or squirrel. Unlike roots, branches are not required for life, but a tree, much like a person, is less attractive, appealing, interesting, or varied without them.

Metaphorically, your branches are how you reach out, what you embrace, and what you hold up. In this way, your branches are extensions of yourself, especially your relationships, and connections with and support of others. Your branches form and inform you. Examples of personal branches include your relationships with family, friends, neighbors, and acquaintances. Examples of workplace branches include your professional relationships and collaborations as well as any networking and mentoring relationships you may have developed.

In what ways have you, as a professional, formed, shaped, and extended yourself through relationships? How have you connected and interconnected with others? What networks have you formed? In what ways have you benefited from collaborating with others? How do you think that others have benefited from collaborating with you? What else would you consider as comprising your branches?

experience branches imaginatively

Imagine a reaching and stretching outward and upward, ever approaching the source of light. Allow yourself to reach and stretch and feel the support of your torso, the straightening of your spine. Feel a release in your shoulders, a lengthening in your arms and wrists and fingers. How far can you imagine stretching your spine and arms? Become aware of the top of your head—your crown. A tree also points upwards with its crown.

Imagine buds waiting patiently throughout the leafless winter in order to sprout in the spring. Did you know that trees grow wider when buds sprout along their branches to form new twigs, leaves and flowers opening toward the light? Did you know that trees also grow taller as new branches emerge above the trunk at the crown to maximize the exposure of leaves to the sun's energy?

Imagine a framework of branches, narrowing as they extend. Witness these branches holding up leaves or needles to receive light and warmth, oxygen and moisture and to enable photosynthesis. Observe these branches growing thicker and sturdier to support more buds, more branches, more leaves, and fruit. Whether they're adorned or unadorned, these limbs reflect and define the season.

From microscopic organisms to fleeting birds to furry mammals, imagine branches protecting, sheltering, housing, feeding, sustaining. Imagine insects swarming, life emerging from hatched eggs, and the staccato searching of a woodpecker. Imagine branches weighted with a playhouse or swing. Imagine branches used for fuel or building material. Imagine continuous growing, extending, offering, renewing.

How have your branches grown? How has your branching network connected and interconnected with others? Have collaborations extended your branches and/or the branches of others? What patterns do your seasonally bare branches trace against the sky? What comprises the leaves that decorate your growing branches?

 *What characterizes your most satisfying working relationships and professional connections?*

Our sense of engagement and satisfaction at work results in large part from the hundreds and hundreds of daily interactions we have while there, whether with a supervisor, colleagues, or customers. The accumulation and frequency of positive versus negative moments largely determines our satisfaction and ability to perform; small exchanges—a compliment on work well done, a word of support after a setback add up to how we feel on the job.
Daniel Goleman (279)

Nourish your connections. Our very sense of fulfillment and satisfaction in life depends on how rich our relationships are. The more socially intelligent you are, the better time you have with the people you love the most—and everyone else, for that matter.
Judith Stone (256)

Networkers expand their sphere of influence by forging alliances and making connections among vastly different groups of people.... Social flexibility and empathy that enables one to find communality with others who might not at first seem to be potential friends, allies, or confederates.... bring information—or power—and inspiration to disparate groups of people.
Caroline Myss (398-99)

As you consider the botanical function of a tree's branches and the metaphorical applications of branches to your career, allow yourself to breath slowly and deeply for a moment. On an exhale, begin to contemplate the question: *How did I develop my most satisfying working relationships and professional connections?* Does a ready answer come to mind for you or do you foresee yourself choosing to engage in a deeper exploration of your professional relationships?

In our botanical metaphor, the branches of the system are interpersonal connections, including mentoring or collaborative relationships. It has been said in the field of organizational development as well as in many others that *everything* is about relationship. Consider your professional relationships and the roles others have played in your professional functioning, successes, and personal satisfaction. It may be that interactions with others in the workplace are the primary factor driving you to contemplate a change or creating reluctance to do so. What kinds of interactions with co-workers do you prefer on a daily basis—frequent, spontaneous, restricted, scheduled? Are feedback and affirmation important to you or are you more comfortable with internal acknowledgement?

Every social interaction at work, no matter how trivial, confirms your place in that community and your identity as a community member. Whether superficial or meaningful, healthy or toxic, the workplace is also a social network. In fact, for many, due to time constraints, inertia, or other reasons, it is the central or most vital source of social interaction. As such, many retirees underestimate the importance of professional contacts, and many who change careers regret doing so because the new social setting is less satisfying than the old, even when the position itself is more desirable.

Consider the qualities of your most satisfying professional relationships—those that are particularly reciprocal, stimulating, and enjoyable. Bring to mind particular interactions, working relationships, and collaborations. What distinguishes them from less satisfying interactions? What do you notice about communication styles, body language, eye contact, positive affect, sociability, rapport, mutual affirmation, task orientation, congruence of priorities? What do you know about your own social skills and preferences? What kinds of relationships would you like more of? How will you deliberately create such relationships in your next stage?

In addition to what is personally satisfying about particular interpersonal interactions, consider what has supported you in your professional growth and development. What kind of support do you prefer from a supervisor—close direction or self-determination? Have you had supervisors or colleagues who have recognized and encouraged your strengths? Have you been mentored? Have you mentored others? What kinds of support would you like more of? How will you deliberately create such support?

I like to consider the function of "mentoring" very broadly—as an interpersonal dynamic in which one individual transmits to another information or an experience that is useful, inspiring, or life-changing. The individuals may be in hierarchical or lateral relationship, and the dynamic may occur once, intermittently, or consistently over time. And, the individuals may exchange roles during or among interactions. The transmission may be through words, ideas, a point of view, insight, guidance, affirmation, emotions, or actions.

Actually, I prefer the term "collaborative relationship." A collaborative relationship is based on mutual respect and cooperation. While power and responsibility may shift back and forth during the course of the relationship, they are vested equally among the participants. And, because each participant expects to offer and receive value, collaborative interactions are mutually beneficial. Thus, the goal of a collaborative interaction is to open a dialog in which participants are equal partners in learning and problem solving and are enabled to perform more effectively and efficiently in future endeavors. The relationship is therefore beneficial or empowering for all participants.

The collaborative relationship is particularly dynamic across generations. If older professionals view the younger as experts in the perspective of their own generation, life experience, world view, and modus operandi, they will embrace the opportunity to gain that insight. Although the younger colleague may fail to recognize or acknowledge the parallel opportunity, with the grace of maturity, the older can simply accept from the other without any need for apparent reciprocity.

Bring to mind the collaborative relationships in your experience. What characterizes them? What distinguishes them from other professional relationships? What distinguishes them from some personal relationships? Did they occur deliberately or serendipitously? How are you likely to establish collaborative relationships in future?

A satisfying working relationship for me is characterized by mutual respect and willingness to both listen and share. I enjoy casual, even playful, interaction, and at the same time I wish to be taken seriously and, in turn, I honor the other. I value true collaborative efforts because I find that different perspectives and varying ideas can create a new whole that surpasses the individual parts. I observe colleagues who prefer to take a more directive role, and that serves well in some situations. Other colleagues are not comfortable speaking in group settings, but may offer suggestions and ideas through one-on-one conversations or via email.

I enjoy collaboration and constructive conversation so much that I am already creating opportunities to get together with others for project development outside of the workplace. For example, I started a landscape committee for my homeowners association and cofounded a monthly gathering at my public library for women in the second half of life. I know that my post-academic activities will include the kind of creative collaborative efforts that are so important to me in the workplace. I truly love branching out in all areas of my life. I appreciate the opportunities my career has afforded me to do so, even as I look forward to new branches that will bear fruit in a new season.

shaping How do you strengthen and diversify your relationships and connections?

Pause again to breath slowly and deeply for a moment. On an inhale, consider the question: *How do I strengthen and diversify relationships and connections?* Does a ready answer come to mind for you or do you foresee yourself choosing to engage in a deeper exploration of your professional relationships?

Most workplaces present opportunities for interaction among people of different birthplaces, generations, political preferences, cultural backgrounds, and interests. If there is strength in diversity, that strength is not realized unless individuals who are aware of differences deliberately seek to understand, respect, and learn from those characteristics that distinguish others. What opportunities have your profession and workplace provided for interacting with varied individuals? What have you learned from those interactions? How have they expanded your perspective?

Consider particular situations in which a synthesis was derived from variant positions. What perspectives contributed to the mix? What process developed for blending them? What advantages were present in the synthesis that would not have resulted from a single perspective? How did you personally benefit from the process? How did the organization benefit from the outcome? How will you foster more such experiences in your next stage?

One point of diversity in many professions is the fact that different generations practice different working styles, which has become the subject of an entire genre of literature profiling the variously named generations. In addition to the many distinctions among generations, there are significant differences between mature and novice professionals. Many professional skill sets accrue over time, including a broad base of experience to draw upon, deeper awareness of possibilities to use in making projections, and familiarity with heuristic models for making choices. Think about what your own maturity or longevity in your profession has afforded you. Are you aware of refined abilities to observe, anticipate, and evaluate? Is it now easier for you to make appropriate choices about conforming or deviating, or to determine potentials for meeting or exceeding desired outcomes?

Perhaps the most significant skill of a seasoned professional is the ability to authentically interact and effectively communicate with a wide range of people. How would you characterize your own interactions with those of different generations? How have you benefited from more experienced colleagues? What opportunities have you created to share your experience with others? How do you think your "wisdom" has been received? How do you think you could improve your skill in sharing experience with others? How will you continue to interact with different generations?

It turns out that, in addition to the obvious social and personal benefits of diverse relationships, there are neurological implications as well. Recent research by Judith Stone, described in Daniel Goleman's *Social Intelligence: The New Science of Human Relationships*, indicates that the "brain as a whole operates more like a social network than a digital computer, with neurons communicating to allow learning and the creation of memory" (251-256). When our outer actions mirror our inner processes, functioning is improved inside and out.

For me, developing effective working relationships and diverse professional connections enhances work life. Because productive social interaction is so important to me, I actively seek out others for collaboration. I have found this often occurs naturally when I demonstrate interest in an issue, idea, or possibility. I have cultivated a problem-solving stance, which can also result in connections. My interest in sharing whatever I happen to be learning at the moment also creates openings for new or deeper connections.

Like most professionals, one way I diversify relationships and connections is by participating in professional organizations. I have also joined other special interest groups. I deliberately seek out individuals who interest me, and I am very interested in other perspectives. Because I like to elicit people's stories, I have developed good listening skills. I practice respect for others, and I am willing to share about myself honestly.

I have noticed my Gen X colleagues, those digital natives, connecting and networking virtually. In the March 2007 issue of American Libraries, Jessamyn West comments about her blogging experience, "how many amazing people I've met who have enriched my professional and personal life to a degree I never would have considered possible" ("Mattering in the Blogosphere," 42).

I have sought out role models within my library and the profession, primarily for inspiration rather than guidance. I have also enjoyed collegial mentoring—seeking support and feedback from peers and providing it when requested. One of my pleasures as a senior professional is the occasional opportunity to mentor a student considering or enrolled in library school. Because my profession continues to change so rapidly, I can anticipate some aspects of the future from the interests and competencies they are bringing to the field, once again making such a collaborative relationship mutually beneficial.

I feel grateful for the branches I have grown and strengthened as a professional. It is very evident to me that I have been significantly formed and shaped by the responsibilities, relationships, and developmental opportunities in my career. Once again, my skills are strengthened and my perspective diversified—positioning me to embrace a new season.

For most people, social interaction is a vital component of work life satisfaction. Fellow workers may provide a sense of community or even family, a source of friendships, or just casual, consistent interaction. Studies have found that even negative or otherwise challenging interactions provide some sense of connection that may be missed after retirement. Even if you have a strong social network independent of your career, the overall balance and quality of your social engagement is an important factor in any season of life. How you develop and sustain relationships may be among the most significant considerations for your next season. Take this opportunity to clarify what has worked for you and how you will create such relationships in your new season of life.

You may also wish to recall your experiences of imagining branches in both this chapter and "To Harvest." Now that you have brought your own personal and professional life to the branch metaphor, do you notice any changes as you imagine again the branches of a tree or your own arms and fingers as branches? Imagine what you can now hold and release as a result of the branches you have grown, expanded, and perhaps shed as well as those that have borne fruit.

Acorns

Having read this chapter, what particularly stimulates or energizes you?

What holds the most value for you?

What deliberate process(es) are you inspired to create?

What spontaneous process(es) do you expect you will have the opportunity to allow?

If you underlined, doodled, or journaled as you read this chapter, review that now and notice:

Any meaning evident now that was not apparent as you wrote or drew.

Anything that surprises or particularly pleases you.

Any redundancies or patterns.

Anything you wish to complete or follow up with. When/how will you do that?

Go through this chapter again and respond to the in-text questions. Notice anywhere you feel uncertain, incomplete, intrigued, or pulled, which may provide important clues about how you have yet to fulfill your career...

Ask yourself:

What branches have I grown during my career/life?

In what ways has my career/life branched out?

In what ways would I like to branch out now?

In what ways has my career provided a social system for my life—e.g., professional and social contacts, social activities during and outside of work time, holiday or seasonal events...?

In what ways have I extended myself and been shaped through my working relationships?

What will I take from my branches and cultivate in the next arc of my life spiral? Your answer to this question may suggest an element of the future you are now creating.

How do you wish to benefit from this chapter?

Return to these questions at intervals during your Harvesting process and beyond to notice any changes in your responses.

Stepping Stones

The purpose of exploring branches is to discern how you as a professional, formed, shaped, and extended yourself through relationships; how you connected and interconnected with others; how you benefited from collaborating with others and others benefited from collaborating with you. Your relationships, like branches, mirror your roots; they form you, but are not you. Like your roots, your interpersonal connections nourish and sustain you; and like tree branches supporting leaves, they enable synthesis.

Narrative Journaling

If you were to visually represent the branches of your career/life, what would they look like—size, shape/form, color, texture? How would they be arrayed on the tree and with what background, foreground, etc.? Do your branches need pruning, shaping, or nourishing?

What questions do you have for your branches? What do your branches say to you?

Respond to the following questions without preliminary reflection:
What do I bring to relationships?
What do I give to relationships?
What do I receive from relationships?

In what ways has your career provided a social system for your life—e.g., professional and social contacts, social activities during and outside of work time, holiday or seasonal events…?

Write about mentoring. Some questions to consider:
How did you benefit from being mentored or from mentoring another? Which role suited you best? How do you think others have benefited from being mentored by you?
Who were your mentors? How did they help you? What lessons did you learn from them? What generation were they from? What generational characteristics helped or hindered your relationship?

Have you been a mentor to a younger person? If so, was it a formal or informal relationship? Was there a generational difference in your styles? How did you work through those differences?

Will you create opportunities to mentor or be mentored as you move out of a professional environment? What ideas do you have for doing that?

Have you looked for or found a mentor for your own harvesting or aging process? Do you think that would be useful to you? How so? What questions would you like to ask someone who has gone through the stage you are at now?

Having completed your narrative journaling for this section, look for themes, patterns, unfinished business, questions, regrets, lessons, high points, inspiration, hopes, plans...

Visual Journaling

Create a realistic or abstract representation of branches, and let it speak to you. What questions does it pose? What answers does it suggest? What does it need or want? How does it communicate?

Visually represent the branches of your career as you described above or instead of describing them verbally. Do the same for the branches of your life. How do they relate and interact?

Rapidly sketch a depiction of a tree. On the main branches, write names of individuals throughout your life and career who have mentored or collaborated with you. On branches radiating out from the main branches, add names of individuals who may later have benefited from that same relationship.

Create a collage of branches. Contemplate your collage in the next day or two. What does it suggest? What reaches out to you? What is missing? Is there anything you would like to change? What is particularly heartfelt for you?

Having completed your visual journaling for this section, look for themes, patterns, unfinished business, questions, regrets, lessons, high points, inspiration, hopes, plans...

Interpersonal Experiences

Share with someone about your experiences of being mentored and mentoring as well as your collaborative experiences.

Engage in a conversation about professional and social networks—how you have each developed and maintained networks, and how you will build upon them and create new ones in future.

Workplace Applications

Consider the branches of your workplace—the interpersonal connections and relationships. Are there any contributions you would yet like to make to your workplace that would extend and form its branches? Also consider your own branches within your position, career, or profession. Is there anything remaining for you to do within your career to extend and form your branches?

Write thank-you notes to individuals in your organization who have mentored or collaborated with you.

Create opportunities in your workplace for discussions about cross-generational working relationships, perhaps including mentoring.

Start a mentoring program in your workplace or professional organization.

Mentor someone.

Ask someone to mentor you.

fruits

ripening How do you create completion in your career and life?

reaping How do you celebrate your accomplishments?

Cultivate the tree which you have found to bear fruit in your soil. *Henry David Thoreau*

A man is a bundle of relations, a knot of roots, whose flower and fruitage is the world. *Ralph Waldo Emerson*

I choose to…live so that which came to me as seed goes to the next as blossom, and that which came to me as blossom, goes on as fruit. *Dawna Markova*

Do not be afraid to go out on a limb. That's where the fruit is. *Anonymous*

What is remembered in all our work is what is still alive in the hearts and minds of others. *David Whyte* (178)

While our dominant culture emphasizes surface accomplishments, in our inner gardens the most important work is often the invisible, the work that no one sees, no one knows but you. It's the promise you keep to yourself, the discipline it takes to persevere in something you value. *Diane Dreher* (99)

Our final stage of human development includes the capacity for rapture as our desire to better understand the world helps to make it a better place for those who live on after us. Our moral concerns shift from the behavior of individuals to global relations and humanity's future. If our efforts bear enough fruit, perhaps we will be remembered as wise. We will have left a lasting legacy, and we will have taken our leave with integrity. *Charles D. Hayes* (152)

Fruit, of course, is a favorite food because it appeals to all human senses and is as beautiful as it is delicious and nutritious. Let's continue our exploration of the tree metaphor by considering the botanical and symbolic dimensions of fruit. In the "To Harvest" chapter, we didn't focus on fruit in the imaginative experience of a tree, so let's do so now.

If you were a piece of fruit, what kind would you be? Why? Imagining yourself as a piece of fruit, are you still on the branch, have you fallen to the ground, or have you been picked? If you are still on the branch, how does that feel? Are you in an early stage of development or fully ripe? If picked, by whom? If fallen, what surrounds you and what is likely to be your destiny?

Becoming yourself again, have you ever had a fruit tree in your yard? What are your fondest memories of living with a fruit tree and its offspring? What is your favorite fruit? What are your preferred ways to prepare and eat fruit? Are fruits a staple in your holiday or other special meals? What else comes to mind for you when you think of fruits?

I learned a lot about fruit when I was preparing to write this book. I learned that all trees that flower produce a fruit, whether it is edible or not. Technically, fruit is the flower's ripened ovary containing a tiny ovule, which, when fertilized, develops into a seed. I was interested to learn that the ovary wall becomes fleshy and forms an outer covering in order to protect, nourish, and transport the seed(s). From the tree's point of view, the function of fruit is to provide a vehicle for its seeds. Fruit is essentially an appealing package to entice creatures that are not root bound like the tree to transport the inner seeds and facilitate the reproduction or carrying on of the tree. And, a fruit reaches fruition when its seeds have matured.

As they develop, fruit change color, form, taste, odor, and value over the course of a life span that concludes with the potential for rebirth. Just so, with the growth of bud, blossom, bloom, flower, fruit, seeds, and dormancy, the annual cycle of the tree comes full circle, and with the germination and growth of any seed, a new life cycle can begin.

In the context of harvesting your career, we will, of course, focus on the "fruits of your labors." Before any reflection, what is your immediate response to that phrase? Do you foresee approaching this topic with an eagerness to examine your largess or some trepidation that your yield may not seem significant? As you consider the fruits of your career, notice whether you emphasize those outer achievements easily recognized by others and to what extent you value the more personal, inner satisfactions that your work life has provided.

According to conventional standards, you would count honors, awards, accomplishments, promotions, innovations, etc. as the fruits of your career. For this harvesting process, the fruits of your career include *all* that has sustained and nourished you. Of course, your fruits include legacies that will continue after you leave the workplace and benefit individuals within the workplace, the entire organization, or a larger community. However, we are *also* each our own legacy—and that is the heart of this book and process.

In the "Roots" chapter you reviewed your career and life progressions and identified patterns. The key questions posed included: In what ways are your contributions part of the root system that sustains your workplace, keeping it healthy and growing? What skills have you developed and in what ways have you become an "expert"? What lessons have you learned and what wisdom you have gained from your work?

In "Branches," you explored relationships and collaborations, and you were asked: In what ways has your career/life branched out as a result of your career? What did you give to and receive from your professional relationships? In what ways has your career provided a social system for your life? What have you learned about working with others of different generations and working styles and about cooperation, collaboration, and synthesis?

The answers to these questions and any others that are telling for you suggest the legacies or fruits of your career. In addition, consider those activities you have been held accountable for and those you have accounted for, whether formally in reports or informally in meetings or conversations. Which would you consider the most significant? The most satisfying? When harvesting, be sure to consider those that are intangible, as well as those that are tangible.

Here are even more questions to stimulate your thinking about the fruits of your career. Which of your fruits were low hanging, i.e., natural and easy, and which required the greatest stretch and effort? Which were required or expected and which were above and beyond? What fruits were the results of team effort and which were independent? Which fruits fed your workplace or your profession? What have you and your fruit embodied in your workplace, career, life? Which fed your soul? In what ways are your fruits attractive, nourishing, useful?

As you consider your fruits, observe patterns, progressions, development. What fruits did you stop growing along the way? When? Why? What new fruits were developed over time? How? How satisfying was that? What fruits did you expect or hope to cultivate that never came about? Would you/could you grow them now? Professionally or personally? Now or in retirement? How have you and will you savor and celebrate the fruits of your career?

In the opening chapter I said that *your* bounty would be a complex of results and outcomes, both more inner or personally felt and more outer or recognized by others. Certainly fruits include accomplishments and achievements. However, outcomes that are personally life-enhancing are the most significant for the purpose of harvesting; and the ultimate inner bounty of your career surpasses the sum of each part considered in turn.

While the process of harvesting the bounty of your career includes identifying your "fruits" and considering them in the context of the preceding questions, the larger issues we will focus on in this chapter address the creation of completion and the celebration of accomplishments.

experience fruits imaginatively

Imagine a tree laden with fruit. Imagine the fruit developing gradually but consistently over the course of a spring and summer as rains fall, birds call, the sun warms deliciously, and the air is freshened with the perfumes of flowers. Notice how the branches are weighted by the abundance of the crop. Consider the following as you begin to experience fruit imaginatively.

Fruit provides nourishment. How have you been nourished by your career? How have you nourished your workplace or profession?

Fruit embellishes the tree and provides for the completion and continuation of its life cycle. How have you embellished your career, and how will you provide for its completion or extension into the future?

Fruit are versatile. Imagine fruit in a basket, in a bowl, in a salad, in a dessert, in a jam. In what ways have you been served by your career?

Fruit are produce. Consider what you have produced as a professional. Of what you have produced, which do you expect or hope will be legacies?

Fruits are the issue, offspring, progeny, or scions of the tree. Have you had the opportunity to grow any successors to your position?

Fruit appeals to all the senses. Imagine holding a piece of your favorite fruit. Feel the size, shape, texture, and temperature. Inhale the fragrance and taste the juicy sweetness. You can even imagine the sound of your satisfied slurping of the last drops.

Which of your senses have been satisfied in your professional endeavors? Which will you indulge more completely in your next stage of life?

Contributions, accomplishments, achievements are examples of professional fruits or legacies. What else would you consider as comprising your fruits?

ripening *How do you create completion in your career and life?*

As you consider the botanical function of a tree's fruit and the metaphorical applications of fruits to your career, allow yourself to breathe slowly and deeply for a moment. On an exhale, begin to contemplate the question: *How do I create completion in my career and life?* Does a ready answer come to mind for you or do you foresee choosing to engage in a deeper exploration of your professional fruits?

Before you move on to your next season, or perhaps in order to move on, consider the completeness of your current stage. Returning to the career and life reviews you worked on in the "Roots" chapter, sort out what feels complete and what feels incomplete. You may wish to begin with relationships. Have you been able to communicate your appreciation to those who have influenced, supported, or inspired you? Have you resolved any languishing misunderstandings, disputes, or ill feelings? Have you been available to support and encourage newer colleagues? Are there any relational bridges you have intended to build? Is there anything you wish to teach or impart to younger colleagues? Would you like to extend yourself as a mentor?

Consider how you enter and end any recycling segment of time—a particular time of day, an hour, a day, week, month, season, year (calendar or academic), decade, or stage of life. Notice if there are patterns in how you tend to enter and conclude any bound segment of time or activity, including reading a book or chapter. What are your patterns of entering into, moving through, and culminating life stages? Have you noticed how some significant and forward-moving phases repeat, such as "the terrible twos," which often reprises at adolescence, and the angst of the late teen, which often repeats in the late thirties and late fifties? Or, how about the parallel that exists between the ages of 21 and 60? Are you aware of challenging phases in your youth that seemed to recur in later decades?

What might nourish and sustain you in your current cycle? What is likely to arise for you that can be supported by positioning it within the perspective of a pattern? Think about the skills and perspectives that are available to you now, which may not have been available at all or may have been less developed in previous cycles. What skills, wisdom, perspective do you intend to develop or enhance as a result of the process being created by this cycle?

I have noticed that I usually enter into a delineated time period or task with a sense of great expansiveness and broad intention. However, I tend to conclude time periods in a narrowed, breathless frenzy to cram in as much as possible. This pattern even plays out when I write letters or inscribe cards. My script begins spaced, large, and flowing and ends tight, tiny, and compacted as I discover that I have a lot more to say than I anticipated. I often run late because I embark upon the time period for departure preparations at a leisurely pace, only to move more and more quickly, as I simultaneously think of more and more details I want to handle before actually leaving.

What I have learned from this pattern is that I am well served by noticing my pace to determine if I am unconsciously dawdling or cramming. I may need to prompt myself for greater efficiency at an outset in order to provide some slack at the conclusion, and I may require some deep breathing to move more easily through a crammed ending. It also helps me to think about the measured, consistent growth of trees and development of fruit—naturally occurring processes that are never rushed and always perfect given the circumstances.

Reflect upon your career as a time segment and consider how you entered your career, and, if applicable, consider how you concluded your career. Would you describe your career entry and conclusion as true to form? If you are not already retired, you will be able to apply your experience of this book to create a conscious, satisfying conclusion, in either a typical or deliberately uncharacteristic fashion. If you haven't yet, you may be ready now to begin projecting some options from which you can make choices over time. The opportunity to write this book has positioned me to create a more mindful career transition. Will the reading of this book do so for you?

Another aspect to consider about cycling through time periods is *what occurs between* every entry and conclusion. What is embraced, relinquished, or transformed? We may embrace what we most desire in any given moment, or we may simply repeat actions of habit or situational requirements. Conversely, we may finally let go of some burden or lose something or someone of great value. As I see it, any given moment may be transcendent or disintegrative.

Your choice to engage with this book indicates your desire for integration and your willingness to consciously honor your transition through your current autumn. In the book, *Harvesting Your Journals*, the authors, Rosalie Deer Heart and Alison Strickland, ask: "How do you define *transition*? How do you know if you are in the midst of one? What lessons have transitions brought you? If you were offered one hour to speak to your grandchildren about transitions in your life, what would you say? What do your dreams tell you about transitions?" (141). Your psyche may very well acknowledge this transition with both night and day dreams. You can respond by using your journal to record and consider such dreams.

Anticipation of and the immediate response to a significant life transition are likely to include both sides of excitement—the thrills and the fears. With this career shift, what are the thrilling aspects for you? What are the scary sides? How have you addressed the duality of excitement in other life situations? What supported you in those situations? What fostered your successful advances? How will you now incorporate what you have learned about what supports and advances you? Simply acknowledging and honoring any ambivalence may soothe you. Or, perhaps you have confidants with whom you will share feelings and concerns.

If you imagine a transition as a deep ravine or canyon intersecting a pathway, there are many options for traversing the chasm—or not. Of course, staying where you are, which often means feeling "stuck," is one option. Some—probably the long-legged—may straddle the ravine. Others may leap precipitously, only to crash and burn at the bottom of the chasm. The cautious may climb slowly down one side and back up the other, while bold ones will leap across gracefully and advance. Still others make the leap, but then get stuck once across. I have found that building a bridge, especially one that incorporates an initiation period and/or ritual, can be a satisfying option. We must take care, however, that the construction process actually moves us forward in a timely manner and doesn't become an end in itself. How do you picture yourself confronting this metaphorical canyon?

What bridges, initiations and/or rituals have you previously created for yourself? What will support your current transition? How do you plan to honor, celebrate, or share this change? What fruits of your career may serve you in this change and beyond?

When I am ready to complete, I look for a felt sense of closure. I take note of any restlessness, distraction, or sense of readiness to move on. I focus mindfully on writing final reports and the organizing, clearing, and filing that signals the conclusion of a project. When I recycle, store, or delete material no longer in active use, I often use the occasion to reorganize or rearrange my office, perhaps including decorative items unrelated to the completed project. I feel refreshed after a process of cleaning out—whether a drawer, a bookcase, computer files, or my entire office. Sometimes I even notice that I have entered that mode before I am explicitly aware that in fact I AM completing!

I also look closely for any loose ends—from unanswered messages to projects that were put on the "back burner" so long ago, they were nearly forgotten. I double-check that items on lists have been addressed and, rather than just let some slide, I prefer to acknowledge any that will be handled late or never.

In these ways, I build a bridge that also creates a rite of closure. Indeed, I enjoy gathering, preparing, and savoring the fruits of any professional project or life phase.

reaping *How do you celebrate your accomplishments?*

Because we live in a society that has lost many traditional initiation rituals, we have lost the ability to recognize the signs that foreshadow transition—our modern term for initiation. We may realize that we are going through a transition, or that we are changing. But because we are unfamiliar with initiatory rites, we do not perceive that we stand at the gate. We do not comprehend that we need to open it and do the threshing and integrative work that are required. ***Angeles Arrien*** (10)

Rituals are not techniques for doing something, but rather lenses through which we magnify the experience of something we are living through. Rituals of passage are simply a way of focusing and making visible the natural pattern of dying and renewal that constantly operates throughout the universe. ***Betsy Kyte Newman*** (17)

Take a moment to breathe slowly and deeply. On an inhale, ask yourself: *How do I celebrate my accomplishments?* Does a ready answer come to mind for you or do you foresee choosing to engage in a deeper exploration of this theme?

As you well know, becoming a professional requires a choice and advance preparation. Entry into a career usually involves an "initiation" period provided by the workplace and followed by a period of development. If we change a job or career, that process may repeat in a meaningful way, or we may neglect to honor the magnitude and significance of the change. However, for the transition from career as a lifestyle, we must generally provide our own rite of passage, because it merits much more than a farewell or retirement party. When you think about it, you may realize that such a transition is no less than a death of what has been and a birth of what will be.

An initiation or ritual might be an event, a period of time, or simply an inner acknowledgment that you are ready, willing, and committed to the next step of your life. At its best, a ritual provides a safe container to move from one life stage to another and a personally meaningful celebration of the passage.

What rites of passage, initiations, rituals, and celebrations are the most meaningful and valuable in your life? Take a few moments now to recall the details of some of them. What distinguishes the best of them from others that were less special? Were the best brief or extended? Planned or spontaneous? Social or private? If social, who participated? What occurred? Were they photographed, taped, or recorded in any fashion? By whom? What makes them memorable?

As a result of harvesting your career, you may discover that you will be better served by a period of transition in addition to or rather than a discrete event. Sometimes an interval of time is required in which we embrace emptiness in order to release the clutter of all previous thoughts and conclusions and allow the gestation of transformation. A Buddhist might say a time of "no name" or of "not knowing." The autumn of a career is a fertile time to enter into the spaces between your activities, words, and expectations. A time to create a brief and temporary suspension of doing and growing new things in order to renew your own acquaintance, look into the mirror of your work life, and discover how you have become who you are. A time to consciously determine who you are becoming. You might even choose to simply remain ripe for renewal, ever a work in progress.

For many, the notion of "not doing" or simply being may be an elusive spiritual goal or just plain unthinkable or unimaginable, perhaps bringing to mind a passive or even vegetative state. In *Jubilee Time*, Maria Harris says, "Being is not equivalent to withdrawal from life. Instead, Being concentrates life in a powerful center point, as a magnifying glass concentrates sunlight on paper, igniting the paper into flame. Being is the state of grace entered by the wise old…who have forgone frenzied activity and busyness" (197).

As you review your career and life, you may discover an unexpected joy in contemplating the completion of many arcs and even the completion yet to come of an entire life cycle. How will you celebrate the completed arcs of your spiral, the fruits of many seasons? You may find satisfaction in considering that ultimately you will fulfill and culminate a rich and varied life comprising a complete cycle, much like a perfect piece of fruit.

One of my friends has created a dynamic and varied life. She always seems to be fully present and satisfied in every endeavor, and yet some part of her always remains alert to new possibilities. She has been recruited for new positions and new jobs repeatedly and relishes each new phase. She creates closure by moving forward quickly with gratitude for both the old and the new. She loves to celebrate each transition with a big party, and her many friends are always delighted to be on hand to congratulate her.

Although I enjoy acknowledging accomplishments with friends or colleagues, as an introvert, I most enjoy celebrating within. I may create a mini-retreat by cloistering myself for an afternoon or taking an extended solo hike. I also journal and reread journal entries to identify demarcations in time and patterns over time. I like to distill and synthesize my self-observations and conclusions, which is how I bring to fruition what I am learning. I create celebration with appreciation, and I welcome the flow of moving onward, just as I welcome the fruits of each season.

Any career transition is a significant life event. Awareness of how you have successfully completed and joyfully celebrated previous life transitions may suggest a rite of passage that will carry you across this threshold and into a season of grace. Just as fruits delight all the senses even as they nourish, you can plan to create a celebration of your career and your self that will both delight and sustain you.

Acorns

Having read this chapter, what particularly stimulates or energizes you?

What holds the most value for you?

What deliberate process(es) are you inspired to create?

What spontaneous process(es) do you expect you will have the opportunity to allow?

If you underlined, doodled, or journaled as you read this chapter, review that now and notice:

Any meaning evident now that was not apparent as you wrote or drew.

Anything that surprises or particularly pleases you.

Any redundancies or patterns.

Anything you wish to complete or follow up with.

Go through this chapter again and respond to the in-text questions. Notice anywhere you feel uncertain, incomplete, intrigued, or pulled, which may provide important clues about how you have yet to fulfill your career…

Ask yourself:

What are the fruits of my career?

How have my fruits enhanced my workplace or my profession?

What are the fruits of my workplace?

Are the fruits of my career also the fruits of my life?

Do the fruits of my career, workplace, and life relate or intersect?

Would I perceive a lack in my life without the fruits of my career?

What will I take of my fruits to cultivate in the next arc of my life spiral? Your answer to this question may suggest an element of the future you are now creating…

How do you wish to benefit from this chapter?

Return to these questions at intervals during your Harvesting process and beyond to notice any changes in your responses.

Stepping Stones

The purpose of identifying your fruits is to savor your accomplishments and preserve what you have learned. The only failures in life are those experiences from which you failed to learn anything. Of particular interest in this season of life is what you may consider legacies—significant, beneficial, profound, expansive, or direction-changing— for yourself, others, and/or a larger social context.

Narrative Journaling

Describe yourself as if you were a fruit—real or fantastical. Include the nature of your skin or peeling, your scent, your fleshy inner, whether you are all of one piece or sectioned within, the form of your seeds and how they are dispersed. How is your fruit more than the sum of its parts? How are you more than the sum of your parts? What will become of your fruit? Will it be eaten, preserved, cooked, or? How nourishing or useful is it?

If you were to visually represent the fruits of your career, what would they look like—size, shape/form, color, texture, scent? How would they be arrayed/displayed—in what context or with what background, container, etc.? Which fruits would you select to represent particular accomplishments or categories of accomplishments?

What questions do you have for fruits? What do fruits say to you?

Which of your fruits were nipped in the bud, never ripened, just right, gone to seed, show/display pieces, worth preserving/canning, able to be saved/stored for future use? Did you make any into pies or other dishes? Has your yield been scant, bountiful, or wasted?

Respond to the following questions without preliminary reflection:
What did I bring to my most satisfying accomplishments?
What did I receive from my most satisfying accomplishments?

Create an initiation ritual to conclude the current arc of your career and segue into the next.

Having completed your narrative journaling for this section, look for themes, patterns, unfinished business, questions, regrets, lessons, high points, inspiration, hopes, plans…

Visual Journaling

Create a realistic or abstract representation of fruits, and let it speak to you. What questions does it pose? What answers does it suggest? What does it need or want? How does it communicate?

Visually represent the fruits of your career/life as you described above or instead of describing them verbally.

Rapidly sketch a depiction of fruit, whether still on a tree, lying on the ground, gathered in a basket, or displayed in a bowl. Randomly write on the pieces of fruit brief labels for selected accomplishments in your personal and/or professional life. How does it feel to look at your achievements thus arrayed? Are there more than you expected? Fewer? Are there some you would have liked to be able to include? Are there some you yet plan to complete? Would you like to rearrange or organize the fruit in some other fashion? If so, create a new version or completely different way of visually and metaphorically representing your legacies.

Sketch a flower form that includes buds and mature blooms with petals. Fill in the petals with accomplishments and satisfactions. Fill in the buds with goals or projects that you consider incomplete or unsatisfying. Add another flower and fill the petals with different actions you would have taken (hindsight is always 20/20!) or outcomes you would have liked.

Create a collage that features a variety of fruit and any other images that you are drawn to as you idly think about the fruits of your career and life. Contemplate your collage in the next day or two. What does it suggest? What stands out? What is missing? What would you like to change? What is particularly appealing (pun intended)?

Having completed your visual journaling for this section, look for themes, patterns, unfinished business, questions, regrets, lessons, high points, inspiration, hopes, plans…

Interpersonal Experiences

Engage colleagues in discussions about their contributions to the organization and your organization's contributions to the field and/or society.

Ask one or more professionals to define "legacy," and to recall personal and/or professional accomplishments that fit their own description. Ask if they would now like to refine their definition, how and why.

Share with someone what you each consider the inner legacies of your careers and/or lives.

Share with someone how you each create closure and celebrate accomplishments.

Workplace Applications

Consider the fruits of your workplace—accomplishments, achievements, legacies. Are there any contributions you would yet like to make to your workplace that would add to its fruits?

Consider your own fruits within your position, career, or profession. Is there anything remaining for you to do within your career to ripen, reap, preserve, or use your fruits?

Compile a list of your organization's legacies—internal, to the field, community, or society.

Write a report detailing your organization's legacies—internal, to the field, community, or society.

Organize a celebration of your organization's accomplishments.

seeds

culminating   *How do you 'relinquish' in your career and life?*

cultivating   *How do you germinate a next season?*

Seeds are the tickets to ride.
There's one life behind them all.
One Life, that the seeds grant us entry to.
Seeds are the vehicles, into and through life.
Tony Basilio

There are only two lasting bequests
we can leave our children;
one is roots and the other is wings.
Anonymous

Seeds are roots with wings.
Deborah F Windrum

The creation of a thousand forests is in one
acorn. *Ralph Waldo Emerson*

A seed hidden in the heart of an apple is an
orchard invisible. *Welsh proverb*

Every adversity, every failure, every heartache
carries with it the seed of an equal or greater
benefit. *Napoleon Hill*

The real voyage of discovery lies not in seeking
new places but in seeing with new eyes.
Marcel Proust

Whereas knowledge is something we have,
wisdom is something we must do. Developing it
requires self-transformation.
R. N. Walsh and F. Vaughn in Baruss (63)

I would like to believe when I die, that I have
given myself away like a tree that sows seed every
Spring and never counts the loss, because it is
not a loss, it is adding to future Life. It is the
tree's way of being. Strongly rooted perhaps, but
spilling out its treasure on the wind.
May Sarton

While developing the tree metaphor, I began thinking about and noticing seeds in a new way. As I considered that a seed, despite its generally insignificant, lifeless appearance, contains the embryo of new life and the promise of rebirth, I became enamored of the tiny vessels. I also began to notice the amazing variety of seeds produced by trees. I (re)learned from some basic botany sources that trees reproduce sexually through pollination, and seeds form as a result of fertilization. Seeds are dispersed to insure survival of the specie through many types of locomotion, including those determined by form, such as "hairs," "wings," tiny "parachutes," buoyancy, burrs, spikes, or hooks carried by wind, water, or fauna, and those dependent upon the participation of insects, birds, or animals that may unknowingly carry the seed or deliberately consume it.

The seeds in a tree's flower, fruit, or cone contain and protect an embryonic plant and nourish it with stored food reserves. If a seed finds an appropriate location and then conditions, light, or other triggers stimulate germination, the embryonic tissues form a seedling. The first part to emerge from the seed case is the radicle or embryonic root of the tree. A stem begins to grow above the radicle. When the seedling uses up the stored food reserves, it transitions from germination to a risky period of establishment. Because the young seedling is so vulnerable, most plants must produce large numbers of seeds to ensure procreation.

You are probably aware of many Biblical, religious, and spiritual references to seeds. If you are a gardener, you might think of the cycle of seeking, gathering, collecting, sorting, preserving, and planting seeds. What does come to your mind when you think of seeds? Recall your imaginative experience of seeds in the "To Harvest" chapter.

Consider the seeds generated by life. Hopes and dreams. Interests we intend to pursue. Goals and objectives. Projects that we begin. Skills that we practice. Things we want to acquire or do. The attraction of particular travel spots. Ways we would like to be of service. Traits and attributes we want to develop. Ambitions. Plans. Desires for health, wealth, relationships, happiness. What are some of the earliest seeds of your life? As a child, what did you want to be and do when you grew up? As an adolescent and teen, what did you long for, work for, dream about?

Think about the seeds that you brought to your first professional position and any positions that followed. From what did they originate—life experience, talents or skills, formal or self-directed education, previous work or jobs? How deliberately had you gathered them? How aware of them were you? Which seeds were explicit intentions, goals, or desires? Which did you plant, and which became dormant? Which seeds took root but failed to thrive, and which grew but ultimately withered away? Which grew differently than expected or desired? Which seeds became exactly the plant you intended? Which do you still hope to plant? Which would you like to plant again in different soil? Which seeds would you like to plant again for similar or different results? Which would you like to plant and then offer as seedling to another?

What seeds have you collected and tucked away during your career? What professional activities or accomplishments have seemed beyond your reach? What personal interests have you given scant attention or set aside? What have you longed for more time to pursue or complete? What feels unattended, incomplete, disregarded? What interests and desires have emerged or reemerged for you in the last few years? What fresh hopes or dreams are you noticing now? What are you seeding? What opportunities are available to you now as you continue, set off, or prepare to embark upon a new stage of life?

What better moment to review what you have cultivated thus far, till the soil of your career, and sort seeds to plot new crops. What vision is forming on the horizon of your life's landscape? What seeds will you plant in your self, in others, in the world?

Seeds must be released by the tree in order to germinate. What will you let go of in order to take root in a new season? In this chapter, we will explore your metaphoric seeds in terms of what has been brought to culmination in your career and what you yet desire to germinate. Allow all of these questions to become seeds themselves as you cultivate your experience of this chapter.

experience seeds imaginatively

Imagine seeds. Generally diminutive and bland in appearance, they are most often trivial refuse discarded after consuming or utilizing the more impressive fruit, vegetable, or flower that they occupy. And yet, the seed contains and protects an embryo, which it nourishes until the sprouted seedling completes the stage of germination.

Imagine a seed as matter that is dense, dark, waiting patiently. Almost nothing, and yet everything—life. Embodiment of growth and change. Around the seed are dynamic processes that it is the center of, but not a part of. Imagine its free fall. Then stillness. Then rapid movement and waiting again. Imagine the seed sinking into and embraced by warmth and darkness—only that. Waiting again. Imagine some subtle shift, almost imperceptible but utterly compelling. A cracking, an opening. A movement that seems to be all around, but *is* the seed itself. An expansion. Pure positive potential. Then release, birth. Imagine the seed feeling its way into darkness, knowing not what else there may be, but continuing to open. And expand. Density loosens. Darkness gives way... but to what?

> …What shape
> waits in the seed
> of you to grow
> and spread
> its branches
> against a future sky?
> *David Whyte* (192)

Metaphorically, the seed is antecedent or that which came before; it is also conception and genesis, the basis of life; it is nucleus, kernel, and core; it is origin, spring, source, spark, inspiration. And yet it is also the final stage, termination; a culmination and a new beginning; pure essence and full potential; what remains and what continues.

You are now selecting and planting seeds for your new season of life.

culminating *How do you 'relinquish' in your career and life?*

…if you let go only of the *externals* of the job situations (the office, desk, materials, and people connected to it) but do not let go of the *internal* associations that cluster around it (the emotional attachment to the job, prestige and power, routines and attitudes of your job, your 'professional' identity), you have made only a superficial change instead of a real transition to retirement. The process of 'disidentification,' or the loss of and separation from work identity, is the painful but necessary process that precedes the new phase of your retirement.
Betsy Kyte Newman (162)

In work as in life, we must contemplate the loss of everything in order to know what we have to give…it is the essence of working; the essence of living; an essence that we look for by hazarding our best gifts in the world, and in that perspective, all of us are young and have the possibilities of the young until our last breath goes out. **David Whyte** (244)

As you consider the botanical function of a tree's seeds and the metaphorical applications of seeds to your career, allow yourself to breath slowly and deeply for a moment. On an exhale, begin to contemplate the question: *How do I 'relinquish' in my career and life?* Does a ready answer come to mind for you or do you foresee choosing to engage in a deeper exploration of your professional seeds?

I found myself looking up several words for this chapter. The word relinquish comes from the Latin "to leave behind." Time and again, we are called upon to leave something behind in our life in order to move forward. We leave behind accoutrements of early childhood to start school, comforts of home to live independently, schooling for a career, employment for self-determination. Each transition is a surrendering and a release, a closure of the old and affirmation of the new. We must always experience a death to what no longer serves in order to birth our self into a next developmental phase. Every autumn in life is likely to include bittersweet loss as well as gain.

Most of us experience both small and significant losses or deaths in our career and life. Perhaps you lost some employment or advancement possibilities. Perhaps you chose or felt compelled to let go of some particular projects, clients, or other opportunities. Perhaps some colleagues, supervisors, or staff moved on. What losses do you recall? How did you process them? Is there yet any residual regret or grief? How will you process that?

Most of us resist loss even as we reach for fresh opportunity. Think about what you have relinquished in your life. What apparent losses became inconsequential or irrelevant as you moved on? What skills and expertise that have served you professionally no longer feel meaningful or relevant—no longer seem to serve you and/or your workplace? What professional responsibilities, functions, or privileges do you feel ready to let go of or make available to others? What satisfactions, benefits, and rewards are provided by your career that you are reluctant to forego? As you consider your career transition, what arises for you as "loss"? What is already dead or dying in your career? Will you grieve? If so, how?

I also looked up the word culminate, which comes from the Latin "to crown." A crowning achievement for you may very well be the culmination of your career. An effective culmination will provide opportunities to wrap up, experience a felt sense of closure, and allow integration. What activities, projects, or goals would you like to *advance* before effecting a change? What activities, projects, or goals would you like to *complete* before effecting a change? What is the story you will tell yourself about the bounty of your career as you apply it to your next stage?

If you balance the letting go with reconciliation, which is from the Latin for "making good again," you can generate positive emotions and energy to initiate a new season. You may even find that it is exhilarating to recast your image, redeploy your skills, recreate your role, and renew your life focus. Which of your skills and areas of expertise will accrue more meaning or value in a new setting? What skills and expertise would you like to develop? What experiences would you like to create? What unfulfilled dreams and desires still resonate with you?

Since I am not one to dwell on the past, I quickly look to the future as a way of moving on. I relinquish by clarifying what I have learned, balancing losses and benefits, and creating closure. I particularly find that focusing on appreciation enables me to experience satisfaction with what has been and openness to what will be. The following short poem by William Blake is inspirational to me in this regard:

He who binds to himself a joy
Does the wing'ed life destroy;
But he who kisses the joy as it flies,
Lives in eternity's sunrise.

cultivating *How do you germinate a next season?*

It seems clear from my own interviews, and from all this research, that only self-chosen purposes, projects, and ties with continued personal meaning are important beyond midlife… ***Betty Friedan***

How do we *live our age* as simply as a new time of our life, a new period of our humanness, a new stage? ***Betty Friedan***

The Visionary archetype lets you imagine possibilities that are beyond the scope of your individual life and that benefit all of society. The Visionary brings into view what could be if certain choices are made, or what is inevitable given choices that have already been made. ***Caroline Myss*** (414)

Our work can be a cry of disappointment or the stirring call of a new purpose. The discoveries that accompany a career transformation… are like a compass. Discovering a meaningful purpose and direction strengthens the will and resolve to bring work into alignment with belief—the head with the heart. We gain a new respect for the characteristics of the new science of chaos and complexity by increasing our intuition, our creativity, our connection with others, our calculated risk taking. We realize that security, in the conventional sense, is an illusion, and that success itself must be redefined. ***Helen Harkness*** (*Capitalizing on Career Chaos*, 144)

Every moment the world is renewed, and we are unaware of its being renewed as it remains the same to appearance. ***Rumi***

Pause again to breath slowly and deeply. On an inhale, consider: *How will I germinate a new life stage?* Does a ready answer come to mind for you or do you foresee choosing to engage in a deeper exploration of creating a new beginning?

Germination in an autumn season is about preparing to replant from the superior advantage of the maturity one inevitably acquires from time and experience. When you create a culmination and celebration that includes a pause—time to simply wait and to be—you are allowing the ground of your being to lie fallow. Fallow land is that which has been plowed, but not seeded. Even the earth requires respite to again become fertile for planting. Thus rested and nourished, renewed possibility and energy can arise.

How have you at other junctures in your life provided for the cultivation of new growth and development? You may wish to review in the "Roots" chapter under "What fosters your growth?" your response to the question about what has supported you in your personal and professional development. It may seem as though growth occurred in spurts and as the concluding result of specific actions or activities. In fact, development is a continuous process that we only notice in spurts and following instances of closure. Do you feel any older the day after a birthday than you did the day before? Is a flower a bud one moment and a blossom the next? Does a building turn old after some specific period of time, or has it been aging imperceptibly all along? Does the sun suddenly drop below the horizon at sunset, or has it been slowly sinking since noon? It's fascinating to consider how much change is occurring around us in every moment, but so slowly that it defies our senses, until we arrive at a marker of time that renders it discernable.

If you are beyond the age of fifty, you may be discovering that not only is life not all over, but in an unexpected sense, it is really only just beginning. You have the prospect of a whole new life built consciously upon your fifty plus years of experience, learning, knowledge, and wisdom. How fun to begin again from such a vantage point and broadening perspective!

In *Soul Mapping* (211), the authors ask:

1. What are you not doing now that you would like to be doing?
2. How are you being called into a larger sense of self?
3. What are you needing to say "no" to? What is the "yes" that these "no's" will make room for?

It is often easiest to imagine a future in terms of the past and/or present—the known. You may also want to explore possibilities for reaping or planting seeds in what have been the margins of your life—spaces beyond imposed or imagined boundaries, unmarked areas only dimly perceived in the peripheries—from which the synchronous, spontaneous, or even feral have arisen for you. What possibilities have been softly calling to you? What interests have assumed a secret life of their own? What precious desires are hidden by debris? What deeply inspires you?

You might consider feeding some of your seeds to the birds and imagining their perspective on the metaphoric tree now representing your career.

*How will **I** germinate a next season? Of course, I have had the advantage of writing this book! I can truly say that engaging with the questions and activities as I developed them was illuminating and resulted in the planting of many new seeds. As I described in the first chapter, I typically embark upon any new endeavor with a period of reading and contemplating. In the past I would then set goals and create a plan. One of the joys of my autumn season is a willingness to simply trust and follow the flow. As I review my answers to the seven questions that precede this one, the inner traits that I am building upon and the outer conditions that I am seeking in my next season are utterly obvious. Is that true for you? And, at the same time for me, I look forward to the natural unfolding of my essence, just like seeds that sprout naturally in the spring.*

Acorns

Having read this chapter, what particularly stimulates or energizes you?

What holds the most value for you?

What deliberate process(es) are you inspired to create?

What spontaneous process(es) do you expect you will have the opportunity to allow?

If you underlined, doodled, or journaled as you read this chapter, review that now and notice:

Any meaning evident now that was not apparent as you wrote or drew.

Anything that surprises or particularly pleases you.

Any redundancies or patterns.

Anything you wish to complete or follow up with.

Go through this chapter again and respond to the in-text questions. Notice anywhere you feel uncertain, incomplete, intrigued, or pulled, which may provide important clues about how you have yet to fulfill your career...

Ask yourself:

What has my career seeded in me?

What have I seeded in my workplace or profession?

In my career, what feels incomplete or seems to hold room for growth or development?

What new skills would I like to bring to the job?

In the next arc of my life, what do I want to bring, give, receive?

What will I take from my seeds and cultivate in the next arc of my life spiral? Your answer to this question may suggest an element of the future you are now creating...

How do you wish to benefit from this chapter?

Return to these questions at intervals during your Harvesting process and beyond to notice any changes in your responses.

Stepping Stones

The purpose of considering seeds is to complete what you have cultivated thus far, till the soil of your career, and sort seeds to plot new crops. What vision is forming on the horizon of your life's landscape? What seeds would you now like to plant in your self, in others, in the world? In the next arc of your life: What can you anticipate? What do you choose to nourish? What will you nurture? What do you intend to receive?

Narrative Journaling

If you were to visually represent the seeds of your career, what would they look like—size, shape/form, color, texture? How would they be arrayed/displayed—in what context or with what background, container, etc.? Has your yield been scant, bountiful, or wasteful?

What questions do you have for seeds? What do seeds say to you?

What attracted you to your career or current work?

What now inspires you?

What activities/kinds of activities
>   fully engage you?
>   breathe life into you?
>   fill you with life?
>   enliven you?
>   animate you?
>   spark you?
>   get your sap flowing?
>   bring satisfaction (during and after)?
>   create flow, bliss?
>   bring you into alignment with your best/most authentic/most promising/ideal self?

What are the activities, experiences, conditions, etc. that you most dislike about your current work or workplace, be they more work-related functions or more personal/interpersonal related? What opportunities are there here for life lessons? What gifts may be in the offering here?

What are the activities, experiences, conditions, etc. that you most enjoy or appreciate about your current work or workplace, be they more work-related functions or more personal/interpersonal related? How would you redesign your job just to provide yourself the greatest satisfaction? In other words, write your perfect/ideal job description.

If you are choosing to remain in your career, what are your options in terms of reduced percent time, responsibility emphases/shifts, job sharing, upward/downward mobility, phased retirement, independent consulting, etc.? Compile a complete list of options, and evaluate, weigh, or "try on" each one.

If you are choosing to exit your career, how will you recreate those aspects of your work that are personally nourishing or uplifting in a different environment? For example—consider your social needs. If you are more of an extrovert, will you find the social stimulation you require? If you are more of an introvert, it may still be that you require some degree of social engagement in order to remain active and engaged.

Respond again to these questions posed in previous chapters:
What did I bring to my career/relationships/most satisfying accomplishments?
What did I give to my career/relationships/most satisfying accomplishments?
What did I receive from my career/relationships/most satisfying accomplishments?

Return to the "Fruits" chapter if you completed the experience of describing yourself as a fruit. What does that fruit want you to do with it next? Would it prefer to be eaten, preserved, arranged? Would it like you to plant its seed(s)?

Return to the narrative journaling experiences of the "Roots" chapter. List the traits that are identified or described in any autobiographical writing exercises that you completed.

If you conducted any life review in the "Roots" chapter, consider it now. Outline, summarize, extrapolate from or conduct a meta-analysis of that material.

Having completed your narrative journaling for this section, look for themes, patterns, unfinished business, questions, regrets, lessons, high points, inspiration, hopes, plans...

Visual Journaling

Create a realistic or abstract representation of seeds, and let it speak to you. What questions does it pose? What answers does it suggest? What does it need or want? How does it communicate?

Visually represent the seeds of your career/life as you described above or instead of describing them verbally.

Rapidly sketch a depiction of seeds or seed packets. Fill in the individual seeds or the labels on the seed packets with future goals and desires.

Create a collage of seeds or things that sprout from seeds. Contemplate your collage in the next day or two. What does it suggest? What stands out? What is missing? What would you like to change? What would you like to further?

Create a three-dimensional seed packet or draw one. Over time, add to it representations of 'seeds.'

Having completed your visual journaling for this section, look for themes, patterns, unfinished business, questions, regrets, lessons, high points, inspiration, hopes, plans...

Interpersonal Experiences

Discuss with others some of the best and worst scenarios for futures in your workplace, profession, personal lives, or the world. Brainstorm alternative projections.

Share with someone how you might each fulfill, continue, or create anew your careers.

Gather with others to create "future maps," for example, with collages.

Workplace Applications

Consider the seeds of your workplace—long-term goals and objectives, plans, vision statements. Are there any contributions you would yet like to make to your workplace that would plant, cultivate, or harvest seeds?

Consider your own seeds within your position, career, or profession. Is there anything remaining for you to do within your career to plant, cultivate, or harvest seeds?

If your workplace has a vision statement, review and update it.

If your workplace has a succession plan, review and update it.

What projects are planned for your workplace's future that you can contribute to now?

Consider establishing a program that will nurture future professionals in your workplace or field, such as scholarships, internships, shadowing…

How else would you like to shape or contribute to the future of your work place?

your harvest

gathering
What social and internalized conditioning led to each of your career choices so far?

preparing
What heart-based inner promptings do you now choose to guide your next life stage?

… the harvest of youth is achievement, the harvest of middle age is perspective, and the harvest of old age is wisdom. *Angeles Arrien* (168)

Wisdom looks to see the jewel of flower shining beyond unexpected places or secured positions. *Spanish proverb*

There is nothing noble in being superior to some other person. True nobility comes from being superior to your previous self. *Hindu Proverb*

Could it be that our most healing work is not to *change* who we are, but to truly *be* who we are? *Rosalie Deer Heart and Alison Strickland* (186)

It's never too late to be what you might have been. *George Eliot*

And then comes the knowing that in me there is a space for a second, large, and timeless life. *Rainier Maria Rilke*

Just as the life that pulses in our bodies goes back to the beginning of the Earth, so too does that heartbeat carry the pulse of those to come after… Given the power of that life that links us, it is plausible to me that these future generations want to lend us courage for what we do for their sake. *John Broomfield* (178)

Don't ask yourself what the world needs. Ask yourself what makes you come alive, and then go and do that. Because what the world needs is people who have come alive. *Howard Thurman*

Focus more on your desire than on your doubt, and the dream will take care of itself. You may be surprised at how easily this happens. Your doubts are not as powerful as your desires, unless you make them so. *Marcia Wieder*

Before we address the culmination of this book—*your* harvest—let's consider one more part of the tree. Covered and protected by a living outer shell or bark, the trunk or bole is the core structure of a tree, arising from the roots, supporting the branches, and protecting life-giving functions. Imagine veins of sap coursing through the trunk—lifeblood that can also become precious external substances—syrup or amber. Think about the trunk as stem, center, holder, and support, providing height to optimize exposure to sunlight for photosynthesis. In many trees, the trunk embodies a record of seasons, climate, and time. Consider how the trunk provides sustenance and shelter for a variety of life forms.

What is the core of you, providing both continuity and possibility? What aspect of your being has thrived upon your roots to extend yourself to others professionally and to manifest outcomes, accomplishments, and achievements in your work and life? What is your essence that will inspirit your continuous unfolding?

gathering   *What social and internalized conditioning led to each of your career choices so far?*

As you consider the botanical function of a tree's core and the metaphorical applications to your career, allow yourself to breath slowly and deeply for a moment. On an exhale, begin to contemplate the question: *What social and internalized conditioning led to each of my career choices so far?* What have you gathered—especially beliefs and assumptions—that you have not questioned? Does a ready answer come to mind for you or do you foresee choosing to engage in a deeper exploration of your core?

I often feel challenged in my own attempts to strip away conditioning and habits in order to perceive my essential self. I try to unearth my essence by asking myself frequently if particular impulses, desires, or aversions are arising from social or internalized conditioning. When I notice that some action or behavior is in fact a conditioned and mindless reflex that doesn't truly resonate, I consciously choose a different course based on awareness and alignment with inner knowing. When I do choose deliberately and authentically, I often notice a shift or expansion of my perspective.

Let's explore the profound nature of one's perspective. A perspective is, of course, a way of looking at life—a frame of reference and a predetermined way to interpret data, events, and behavior. It provides a context and a set of criteria with which to evaluate experiences and make choices. To my mind, a perspective is neither wrong nor bad, although a particular action or behavior derived from or in response to a particular perspective may be judged as bad or wrong by others.

We all function from a perspective based upon individual life experiences and exposure to a culture and transmitted viewpoints. Groups, organizations, ideologies, religions, and political parties each offer a circumscribed worldview that is intended to be held in common by followers or members and to inform each individual's perspective. Your personal point of view is your own unique set of beliefs, expectations, assumptions, and attitudes that comprise a lens through which you observe and interpret your world.

To enter into this concept, try imagining your life as a climb up a massive redwood tree—one that is so high, its crown is not even visible from the ground. As a young child at the base of the tree, everything you can see is on the same level, and it is difficult to see very far or to differentiate very clearly. One way to cope with this limited perspective is to keep your focus pretty close to yourself and your immediate surroundings, which are familiar, comfortable, safe, most easily discerned and related to, and certainly the most important to you. Then, as you begin climbing the tree, both your view and your capacity to take in and relate to what you see expand.

As each of us climbs a metaphorical tree, we form associations with parts of it. The roots may feel like someplace we wish to remain for as long as possible or someplace we can't leave quickly enough. The crown may appear ever-inviting or shrouded in ominous clouds, mysterious and foreboding. And, as we travel upward, there may be branches that similarly appeal or repel. Places we wish never to leave or do never leave. Places we circumvent, avoid, or deny. Places we always recall with distaste or shame, or deliberately or unconsciously forget. Places where we linger or that we remember forever with particular affection. Whatever your experience, your ability to acknowledge the key influences along your journey will provide great insight into your current worldview.

On way to identify influences is to imagine that caretakers, family, friends, church, school, community, and media offer or insist that we use metaphorical viewfinders, that is, predetermined concepts, contexts, rules, ethics, codes through which to perceive and interpret what we see and observe. As you know, a camera viewfinder is what you look through to focus and compose a photo. Our metaphorical viewfinders also determine where we look, what we perceive, and how we feel about what we believe we see. Although they enable sighting, they also limit our view.

We all accept and discard some quantity and variety of viewfinders as we make our way up the redwood. Some of us accept a dominant viewfinder and appreciate climbing the tree with a clear, consistent, time-honored device that is perceived as the truth and that serves our purposes well. Others are always dissatisfied, restless, and seeking a better viewfinder. You may know someone who is always joining some "Viewfinder-of-the-Month" club—hoping that the right viewfinder will prove to be a panacea, ultimate solution, or THE answer. Personally, I enjoy the process of seeking out and experimenting with a variety of viewfinders in order to discover the most satisfying views and ways of looking at them. How would you characterize your own experiences with viewfinders?

As we progress up the redwood, we each use our viewfinder to perceive not only the environment we are traversing, but also the view from higher branches. One of the gifts of maturing and moving upward is the opportunity to perceive an ever-widening view—with greater or lesser focus and clarity, depending on our awareness and the extent to which we have developed our ability to notice. Our perspective is not just what we see, but also how we have learned to see, and it is made complete with our awareness of what is determined by our viewfinder.

A perspective is difficult to evaluate, or even to recognize as such, from within the structure of its tenets. Try to stand apart from or outside of the circumference of your perspective even just briefly in order to distinguish the contents and the container, the relationships between the parts, and the relationship of the whole to other containers or possibilities. Doing so, you may be able to start sorting out the conditioning that has been imposed from outside, the conditioning you have internalized, and your heart-based inner promptings and knowing.

Among the questions that may assist you in this process, consider: What prompted your career choices? Money? Status? Parents or spouse? Personal dreams or goals? Location? Inertia? Guilt? Serendipity? Health issues? Desires to stretch and grow? "Shoulds"? Opportunities to travel? A heartfelt desire to help others? A compelling sense of social responsibility?

Identifying the driving forces behind your career choices enables you to perceive the worldview that informed them. How has your perspective changed over the years as you ascended higher in your redwood? Is a shift in perspective now prompting your consideration of a shift in career? Is your current position closer to the treetop affording a view that is awe-inspiring? Perhaps you are ready to release the use of a viewfinder and learn to trust your own unmediated vision?

Among my women friends, some felt driven by a desire for "success" and goals that demanded a relentless ascension up a single career ladder. One friend became exhausted and sick after many years in the high-stress job she had dreamed of since childhood. She eventually left the big city where her company was headquartered and invested her savings in starting a bed and breakfast in a beautiful mountain location. Another friend spent many productive years in the career her parents had preferred, until she quit to realize her own passion, despite the required years of education and training that diminished her financial security. Other friends, motivated by an inner quest for self-fulfillment, pursued a variety of working and self-employed situations.

When I ask myself what social and internalized conditioning led to each of my career choices, I realize that I felt compelled to have a career for both social and personal reasons. Coming of age in the time of "women's liberation," I felt strongly about being an independent, self-supporting woman. I wanted the status, as my mother never had, of working outside the home. Busy, engaged career women impressed me, and I felt that I needed a career for self-esteem and life satisfaction. Although I considered great wealth suspect, I did desire the material comfort and security that seemed to be required for a "good" life. I also wanted to exercise the strengths and skills I had developed as a successful student.

I experimented with social work and English literature as career choices, but when I started library school I knew that I had found the right field for me. I took my studies seriously, as well as what I was taught about being a "professional." For twelve years, my work was my life.

My professional zeal diminished unexpectedly after I had a baby at forty. I had planned to resume active involvement with campus governance and professional organizations after maternity leave. As a new mother, however, I found such activities far less compelling, and I resented extended hours away from my baby. My perspective had shifted dramatically.

I actually struggled for years trying to balance the demands of family and career. Fatigue and increasingly debilitating physical symptoms in my middle forties forced me to create even more alignment between my well-being and my work. And, in order to dispel the dark cloud that descended in my early fifties, yet another shift in perspective was required, which resulted in writing this book.

I feel fortunate that seemingly outer circumstances forced me to reevaluate values and priorities at key points in my life. As I gained higher footholds in my own redwood tree, the expanding views created shifts in perspective that enhanced my life and deepened my spirituality. The shifts also foster a desire for even broader views and the confidence to continue climbing.

preparing   *What heart-based inner promptings do you now choose to guide your next life stage?*

As you consider the botanical function of a tree's core and the metaphorical applications to your career, allow yourself to breath slowly and deeply for a moment. On an inhale, begin to contemplate the question: *What heart-based inner promptings do I now choose to guide my next life stage?* Does a ready answer come to mind for you or do you foresee engaging in a deeper exploration of your core?

An expanding perspective may very well be the main course you prepare from your bounty. To my mind, it is the ultimate gift and purpose of personal development and maturity. My own perspective expands when I allow myself to simply notice. Noticing, of course, requires presence, mindfulness, inclusivity, and non-judgment. You can choose to notice both what is outside you (your environment, other people) as well as what is inside you (thoughts, feelings, reactions, behaviors).

As you look back at your life, do you sometimes feel as though it has included "other lifetimes"— experiences so long ago, varied, or distinct from each other that they seem to be parts of other incarnations? Decades of such experiences and a conscious, tempered perspective are gifts of maturity. You now have the opportunity to consider events of the present in a rich "historical" context that includes not just the number of years you've existed, but also your life circumstances, education, training, personal and professional development, experiences, relationships, information, knowledge, and wisdom. You may find, as I do, that an expanding perspective is deliberately incremental and fluid.

In the course of your life, you have examined, rethought, regretted, and congratulated yourself on many choices, behaviors, and actions. You have conversed with, listened to, or read many individuals with thoughts and ideas that supported or contradicted your own. You have sustained, rejected, and embraced a variety of ethical, religious, political, and philosophical schools of thought. You make choices daily, both consciously and unconsciously, based on your worldview and your perception of yourself within that view.

As I said above, maturity affords the option to perceive an ever-widening view as you reach new heights in a metaphorical life tree. Like a bird able to ascend, perceive, and travel beyond extensive vistas, you, too, are now graced with the ability to achieve the expansive perspective—the bird's eye view. Consider that your willingness to engage with big pictures using the 20/20 vision of hindsight and the understanding and compassion of life experience will enable you to reinvent the past and the future. Thus, the simple choice to open to a new and fresh perspective can be profoundly liberating.

Sometimes, however, the more mature perspective is actually the more childlike. In a *Slate.com* (April 26, 2007) interview, Alison Gopnick, author of *The Scientist in the Crib: Minds, Brains, and How Children Learn*, says, "For grown-ups, consciousness is like a spotlight; for babies it's like a lantern. I have always loved the childlike moments, however brief, when our minds seem to open to the entire world around us—the experience celebrated by Romantic poets and Zen sages alike. The neuroscience makes me think that these moments aren't just a passing thrill. Cultivating this childlike 'lantern consciousness,' this broad focus, might help make us almost as good as babies at changing our brain."

This "lantern consciousness" can also be used to gaze softly inward with non-judgment, compassion, and an open, accepting heart and to gaze softly outward with the inclusive, reflective, and imaginative skills of the right brain. The perspective of maturity is generally a softening that creates the expansiveness of deepening clarity.

If what brought you to this book is amorphous dissatisfaction, ennui, or restlessness, as opposed to clarity about this being your time to retire and/or change your career, you may even find the passion and courage you require to stay in your career for now with a renewed commitment to professional development, new connections, creative approaches, and a fresh perspective. Or, if you are clear that this is your time to initiate a new season, your responses throughout the book are likely to offer motivation, vitality, confidence, and resolve to do so.

An expanding perspective elevates your vision beyond the needs and wants of your life to bring into view the greater good. Those of us in The Autumn of life may well ask if we are now positioned in life and motivated from within to take action in support of a greater good.

*What heart-based inner promptings am **I** choosing to guide my next life stage? As a result of developing metaphors and questions for this book, talks, and workshops, I am now clear that my primary gift is the ability to create opportunities for myself and others to learn what we already Know within. I am also clear that my path to being a part of the solution on a planetary level is to create opportunities for myself and others to become alive to the satisfaction and imperative of supporting others and the planet. From within I know that it is time for me to step forward into a broader social arena, and I embrace a willingness to take new risks in that endeavor.*

Are you discovering any gap between the conditioning that has thus far influenced your life choices and the inner urges that you may have been neglecting or that may be now coming into focus for the first time? Simply identifying any such gap may inspire choices that will bring your life into greater alignment with your heart. Perhaps the process of harvesting the bounty of your career has prepared you to plant the seed of that alignment.

experience your harvest imaginatively

Having experienced five previous guided visualizations, go inside this time to imagine your own vision of a mature tree laden with fruit or the variegated flags of autumn. Take in everything about this tree in full sensory detail. Notice first the root system anchoring and nourishing the tree. Observe the branches that give it mass and form. See the ripened fruits that weight the branches, lay fragrant on the ground, or have already been gathered. What seeds have been released by that fruit, and which will you pluck for future growth? Consider well the trunk of the tree. How does it protect and reflect the core of the tree? What are you learning about the tree's essence and about your essence?

Having experienced your career in terms of roots, branches, fruits, and seeds, which of these do you think is the most established, developed, highly-functional, nourishing, lush, vibrant, supportive, growing?

Which are the least developed and cultivated? Which are you most interested in developing? Which are the most intriguing for what they could be?

What did you learn that was unexpected about any of them? In what ways do they whisper to you now?

What does this tree have to say to you?

Look around to notice where your tree is situated. Do you find yourself in a garden? Orchard? Wood? Farm? Streamside? Mountaintop? What is the weather like? What time of day is it? What is the season? What is the bird's eye view of this tree? Take in everything about the area in full sensory detail.

Notice before you now in your imagined scene a shiny green wheelbarrow. This wheelbarrow has appeared to facilitate harvesting the bounty of your tree. What will you place in the wheelbarrow? What will you leave beneath the tree? Where will you steer the wheelbarrow? How will you enjoy the bounty when you reach that destination?

Return to the company and inspiration of your tree and its surroundings for as long as wish. When you are ready to move on, allow a new scene to unfold before you, and again, take in everything in full sensory detail.

Notice now that another shiny green wheelbarrow is present. This one is filled with stepping stones. What are they made of? What is their size? Color? Texture? How will you select and arrange them to create a pathway to the new scene and season now before you?

your harvest

In the first chapter of this book, I said that as someone who has invested significant time, energy, and life resources in a work endeavor, you have also endowed yourself with a largess of experience, skills, knowledge, perspective, and discernment—the personal bounty of your career. That bounty is a complex of results and outcomes, both more inner or personally felt and more outer or recognized by others. From my perspective, even more important than any accomplishments and achievements apparent to others are the outcomes that are personally life-enhancing for you. The true bounty of your career surpasses even the sum of the parts you have considered in preceding chapters. The true bounty is the quality of your life force NOW—that which animates you, enlivens you, and makes you radiant.

Many significant experiences in life, whether brief or extended, serve as initiations. Stories of adolescent "coming of age" events describe spontaneous or serendipitous rites of passage. We actually "come of age" many times throughout our life. In what ways are you coming of age now? If you consider your career an "initiation," what have you been prepared for or initiated into?

To fulfill the harvest of your career, allow yourself to breath slowly and deeply for some moments. Briefly recall your responses to the following questions:

1. *What supports me as a professional?*
2. *What fosters my growth?*
3. *How do I develop my most satisfying working relationships and professional connections?*
4. *How do I strengthen and diversify my relationships and connections?*
5. *How do I create completion in my career and life?*
6. *How do I celebrate my accomplishments?*
7. *How do I 'relinquish' in my career and life?*
8. *How do I choose to cultivate a new season of life?*
9. *What social and internalized conditioning led to each of my career choices so far?*
10. *What heart-based inner promptings do I now choose to guide my next life stage?*

Responses to the odd-numbered questions, which you addressed on an exhale, may offer guidance and support for a satisfying culmination of your career. Responses to the even-numbered questions, which you addressed on an inhale, may offer guidance and support for a satisfying next stage.

In addition, consider the following, which are often pointers to impending change:
What are you now dreaming, thinking, talking, reading about?
What synchronicities or serendipities are occurring in your life?
What words, images, symbols, colors, feelings, longings are recurring in your life?
What are your last thoughts at night and first thoughts upon waking?

When faced with change, including a career change or retirement, we may feel particularly adventurous and open to a variety of new experiences. You may now wish to consider an exploration of subjects or activities that have provoked twinges of curiosity or lurked in the corners of your mind. Perhaps there are destinations you have secretly wished to visit or organizations that have appealed to you. Have you maintained a list of books you'd like to read or cultural events you'd like to attend? Are you interested in changing or expanding your social circle?

As you move through this turning point in your life, consider previous transitions that were formative, expanding, transformative. Such defining moments are probably etched into your core, not unlike the knots that add texture and interest to a piece of wood. Self-identified turning points of your inner life are likely to offer more significant markers of your growth than birthdays or a litany of traditional life events. How would you describe your life in terms of a series of inner transformative experiences? How does your current perspective embody each expansion that your life has afforded?

Now that you have arrived at an autumn of life, you may feel ready for a natural unfolding. Ready for your colors to transmute. Ready to allow your essence to be revealed in its bare beauty. Ready for the wise, warm nurturing soil of the earth mother to nourish and sustain you naturally. Ready to open your heart and life to a natural unfolding. Ready to allow the present to unfold in innate knowing and wisdom. Ready to allow your being to softly open to the mysteries and miracles of life lived from the moment. Now is a season for your life to unfold, for you to unfold.

Acorns

What will I now choose to harvest from my career for the next arc in the spiral of my life?

What will I take from my harvest for nourishment?

What else would I like to grow and harvest in my life?

Having read this chapter, what particularly stimulates or energizes you?

What holds the most value for you?

What deliberate process(es) are you inspired to create?

What spontaneous process(es) do you expect you will have the opportunity to allow?

If you underlined, doodled, or journaled as you read this chapter, review that now and notice:

Any meaning evident now that was not apparent as you wrote or drew.

Anything that surprises or particularly pleases you.

Any redundancies or patterns.

Anything you wish to complete or follow up with.

Go through this chapter again and respond to the in-text questions. Notice anywhere you feel uncertain, incomplete, intrigued, or pulled, which may provide important clues about how you have yet to fulfill your career…

How do you wish to benefit from this chapter?

Return to these questions in the future to notice any changes in your responses.

Stepping Stones

To harvest is to gather, sort, and prepare. As a result of engaging with this book, you have gathered in your thoughts, journal, and other containers the riches of your roots, branches, fruits, and seeds. You have sorted this largess to select and distill that which you are now choosing to offer a new season. You have also selected some variety and quantity of stepping stones to create a pathway to that season. What will complete your preparations?

Narrative Journaling

What is your favorite tree? Why? Describe it. How does it reflect or characterize you?

If your career were a tree—what kind would it be, why, what would it look like? You might prefer to describe it out loud into a recorder or to another.

How does your tree view YOU? What do birds or other creatures have to say about your tree? What do other trees have to say about your tree?

In your career, what has been your sunshine, rain, pests, birds, squirrels, diseases, erosion, frost, drought? Have you experienced any fire? Have you had a gardener? Has anyone built a tree house in your branches? Have any birds nested in your branches? Describe the eggs and the life cycle of the nesting birds.

Did your career grow into a tree other than what you thought you were planting? Did it take shape other than what you expected? Did it grow fruit other than what you expected?

If you view your career as a tree, what does it suggest you do next? Fly away as a seed? Cultivate the tree further? Trim and prune the tree? Plant around it? Create a garden around it? Pluck and savor its fruits? Display or sell the fruits? Plant the tree's seeds? Cultivate companion trees? Make art with its branches? Arrange some of the tree's branches or flowers in a vase? Carve the trunk of the tree? Harvest its wood? Grow another tree?

As you consider the patterns of your life and career and a possible new stage, ask yourself:

What can I anticipate?

What do I choose to nourish?

What do I intend to receive?

What will I offer?

In the next arc of your life, what do you want to bring, give, and receive?

Think about one or more individuals you admire, whether you actually know them or not. Write a character profile of one or more of them or list their admirable qualities or traits. The traits we admire in others are latent or already manifesting in our self. Of the traits you have noted, which can you find latent or overt in yourself and which will you deliberately cultivate?

Allow the details of your life to recede and imagine in abstraction the essence of your self and your journey so far. What pictures or images come to mind as you reflect upon your self and your life? What have been and are the dominant colors of your life? Are there key words that capture aspects of your life? Are there images or words that express the opposite of who you are? What are the recurrent tunes, melodies, rhythms, and beats of your life? What about the dream, shadow, or unrealized part of you—like the dark portion of the moon?

Review your entire narrative journal. Look for recurrent ideas or images, themes, patterns, persistent questions, doubts or concerns, the most consistent positive messages. How does your narrative journal enhance your perspective?

Visual Journaling

Create a realistic or abstract representation of a tree, and let it speak to you. What questions does it pose? What answers does it suggest? What does it need or want? How does it communicate?

If you were to visually represent your career as a tree, what would it look like? In what context or with what background would you portray it—in a garden or forest or?

Is there another or better metaphor than a tree for your career? Represent it visually.

Create a collage of trees. Notice the amount of space given over to each part of the tree: roots, trunk, branches, leaves, flowers, fruit, etc. What season is it? What types of trees are included? What is included besides trees? What is the bird's eye view of the collage? Contemplate your collage in the next day or two. What does it suggest? What stands out? What is missing? What would you like to change? What would you like to grow?

If you collaged, bring all of your collages together and notice how they differ, overlap, communicate to each other, communicate to you. What do you most like about the collages as a whole? What do they say to you? What suggestions or advice do they offer? What do they say about you, your career, your life? What next life intentions are manifest in them? Engage with them as one large collage or create a new "Life Map" collage, as suggested by lifestyle makeover expert Cheryl Richardson, who suggests you ask:

- What have I learned about myself from looking at my Life Map?
- Do I see any patterns?
- Does anything on my Life Map surprise me?
- If I knew that all of the images on this Life Map would come to life, would I be okay with that?
- Who do I need to become in order to fulfill the intentions of my Life Map?
- Based on my Life Map, what quality will I commit to developing this year?

Draw some form or image that represents you. Color in one half of the form. What is not yet a part of this picture?

Review all of your visual journaling. What stands out, repeats, is unique, feels incomplete that you would like to complete, feels incomplete that you would not like to complete now? Create a composite visual representation of your experiences with this book and pose the same questions.

Interpersonal Experiences

Share with another what you have gained from this book and your experiences in order to propagate your own seeds and to perhaps plant a seed in that person.

Review all of your interpersonal experiences. Repeat one of them or create your own interpersonal experience and complete it.

Workplace Applications

Review all of the workplace applications if you have not yet completed any of them. Choose one that you really will do and schedule it on your calendar. Or create your own organizational application and schedule it on your calendar. If you did follow through with a workplace application, how would you do it differently now?

a woman's life cycle

MAIDEN · MAKER · MAVEN · MUSE

seasons of a woman's life
the time of your life

Remember when I welcomed you into my home for tea, and we gazed out the window at the unfolding autumn scene and glistening ripe apples? Given the scope of the conversation that followed, do you now find your life unfolding as a result of exploring your roots, branches, fruits and seeds? Has the tree metaphor provided a framework to identify the gifts of your "career" to date and to support you in carrying some of these gifts over to a next stage of your life?

When I completed this process, I found that I was inspired to continue exploring my entire life. And, having connected so deeply with trees as I explored the bounty of my career, I looked again to nature for a metaphor that embodied my life stages. Once I realized that a woman's life could be seen as comprised of four stages, the four seasons was an obvious metaphor.

Are you ready to explore your life course with this metaphor? If so, I think it's time for another cup of tea as we begin to examine your past, present and future as a meaningful cycle.

seasons of a woman's life

The tree, which provides the central metaphor of this book, also provides a classic case study of life in concert with the cycling of the seasons. Fred Hageneder, author of *The Spirit of Trees: Science, Symbiosis, and Inspiration* (51-52), draws on the experiments of mathematician Lawrence Edwards with the leaf buds of deciduous trees to explain.

> Trees, like the whole of vegetation, breathe and pulse in rhythms of cyclic time. During the autumn they draw their essence inwards and compress it in processes which produce the seeds. The leaf buds on the twigs wait all winter for the big day in spring when they, together with the seeds below, open up to the light and the air of surroundings (Edwards, 256).

> During the four or five weeks after the winter solstice the pulsing of plant buds becomes even smaller; the Earth has *inhaled* fully and is waiting. Finally, in the spring, all vessels burst open and unfold. The Earth *exhales* until the full splendor of the summer solstice. Thus, the natural world moves rhythmically, and the movements of the stars are reflected in the ground beneath our feet.

> No cosmic cycle has been identified that might stimulate [the] seven-year rhythm [of trees], but human beings are also influenced by a seven-year rhythm—it takes the human body seven years to replace its cells. The science of Anthroposophy counts the phases of man's inner development in the groups of seven years, and most cultures have divided time into weeks of seven days. We begin to see the world in which we live as a vast organism, in which the roles of planet and plant are intimately interwoven, one with the other. No star can move, but a plant responds (Edwards, 225).

Although there is so little time in our busy working days to cultivate the natural unfolding of our life and honor each stage, most women nonetheless remain at least somewhat attuned to our inner shifts and transitions. What do you think fosters such a felt connection and desire to observe cycles of selfhood and nature? Perhaps it is the sheer physicality of menarche and the relationship of our monthly cycle to that of the moon. Perhaps our lifelong and evolving hormonal urges and drives or the rich possibilities of menopause. In fact, it is often the journey of menopause that causes professional women to notice that the arc of our career extends further behind than before us. And, as we begin wondering what the next arc may offer, we frequently embark upon an inner exploration of our past, present, and future.

Countless tales and myths represent three distinct stages of a woman's life as maiden, mother, and wise woman or crone. The current phenomenon wherein millions of educated, active women are moving through menopause and entering a stage of life that is new both for them individually and for our entire culture is precipitating a cultural shift of enormous magnitude. From my perspective, women in the second half of life are today's pioneers. For the first time in history, we are experiencing a length of time after child-rearing and career-building that promises to be productive, creative, and vital—vital for each of us personally and, I am convinced, vital for the future well-being of the planet. Given that, I think it is time for a fresh and expanded life cycle model.

When Susan and I started creating workshops during the preliminary stages of developing this book, we identified a fourth persona to bridge the stages of mother and crone—that of "maven." Of course we looked it up! Maven is defined by *The American Heritage Dictionary of the English Language* as a "person who has special knowledge or experience; an expert." The term is derived from the Yiddish and Hebrew words meaning to understand and to discern [maven. Dictionary.com. The American Heritage® Dictionary of the English Language, Fourth Edition. Houghton Mifflin Company, 2004. http://dictionary. reference.com/browse/maven (accessed: May 28, 2007)]. And, as I mentioned earlier, recognizing this fourth stage brings the cycles of a woman's life into alignment with the four seasons of the year.

The addition of Maven to the long-standing trilogy of female roles acknowledges that most women will experience at least one other distinct stage beyond those of the young maiden, the reproductive mother, and the elder. Menopause remains a significant transition, and now it is often a passage into a whole new and productive life stage rather than into a stereotyped period of decline and diminishment. Actually, the role of Maven could occur before, during, and/or after that of care taker—whether for a biological or adopted child or children, someone requiring consistent, long-term care, or some significant project or work.

The physical and inner journeys of menopause often release a very different woman and a new, softer mindset towards her self and her life. Since at least the early 1990s when Gail Sheehy was conducting the research for her ground-breaking book *The Silent Passage*, surveys measuring the well-being and happiness of women in their fifties and sixties have shown clearly and consistently that post-menopause often initiates a new life experience of self-acceptance, life satisfaction, and *joie de vivre*. According to neuropsychiatrist Louann Brizendine in *The Female Brain*:

> …'postmenopausal zest' is a phrase coined by anthropologist Margaret Mead. It is a time when we no longer have to be concerned with birth control, PMS, painful cramps, or other monthly gynecological inconveniences. It is a stage of life that is free from many encumbrances and full of wonderful possibilities. We are still young enough to live life to its fullest and enjoy all the good things nature has provided us. Many women experience a renewed zest for life…and look for exhilarating adventures or new beginnings. It is like starting life all over with a better set of rules (142).

Women now transitioning through and beyond menopause are clearing new pathways for themselves, their cohort, and women yet to pass this way. Brizendine continues:

> A century ago, menopause was relatively rare. Even in the late nineteenth and early twentieth centuries, the average age of death for women in the United States was forty-nine—two years before the typical woman ends her menstrual cycle. Women in the United States can now

expect to live many decades after their periods stop. Science, however, hasn't fully caught up with this change in demographics. Our knowledge about menopause is relatively new and incomplete, though it's advancing rapidly as large populations of women are moving through this once rare transition. Forty-five million American women are now [2006] between ages forty and sixty (155).

In *The Second Half of Life*, Angeles Arrien notes, "because of our increased longevity, for the first time in history we…have the opportunity to create a map of spiritual maturity for future generations to use as they enter their own later years" (4). In fact, in *New Passages*, Gail Sheehy cites research by Dr. Leo Stole that concludes, "improvement in mental health and well-being among older women was accumulating generationally" (193). That is, each successive generation of women studied showed increased later-life satisfaction and a higher percentage of women indicating such satisfaction!

In addition to recognizing the important new life stage of Maven, Susan and I wanted to rename the stages before and after Maven. Most women experience the decades of the 20s, 30s, and 40s, but not all experience biological motherhood or any mothering in those decades. During those decades, however, most women find themselves busy making relationships, partnerships, homes, jobs, alliances, and perhaps families—so, we call the woman in her 20s, 30s, and 40s the Maker.

We also reconsidered the fourth stage. The ancient wise woman was perceived as a witch because others misunderstood her knowledge of the natural and the healing, fearing her power and capacity to empower. When I thought about it, I realized that she probably donned black as a widow, and that, of the few people who would have lived to her age, most would have been toothless, bent, and haggard. Although many women are trying to reclaim the word "crone," it remains riddled with negative connotations and images—including ugly, gossiping, and mean. In order to circumvent any such negative associations, Susan and I brainstormed until we came up with the word "muse" to suggest the creative inspiration that a woman in her 70s, 80s, and beyond may provide herself, others, and society when given her due role. The term also, of course, refers to the exercise of humor and contemplation that may characterize the older and wiser woman.

Much is revealed when we overlay these four stages of a women's life with the seasons and the tree metaphor. In our springtime (the March, April, and May of our life), we are indeed the fresh young Maiden, whose focus is on *growing* and whose symbol might be the *bud*. From 0-10 we experience the inhale, or ascent, of *beginning*, like an arising bud; and from 11-20 we experience a deepening descent, or exhale, into *blossoming*. The song of the Maiden is the song of spring: new life, fresh energy, green and golden, opening, growing, reaching. These are the decades of establishing *roots*.

In our summer (the June, July, and August of our life), we are the Maker, whose focus is on *promising* and whose symbol might be the *flower*. From 21-49, we experience many series of inhales and exhales, ascents and descents as we engage in *tending* (our jobs or careers, our home and family) and *befriending* (our selves and others, building our support systems), the very apt terms used by UCLA researchers in their studies of the differences between how women and men handle stress (University of California Los Angeles). The song of the Maker is the song of summer: busy, productive, alive, energetic, glowing, fruitful. These are the decades of growing *branches*.

In our autumn (the September, October, and November of our life), we are the Maven, whose focus is on *fulfilling* and whose symbol might be the *fruit*. We experience the decades of our 50s as a *rising* ascent or inhale, followed by a satisfying exhale or descent in our 60s to *reigning*. The queen mother would be the perfect image of the Maven. The song of the Maven is the song of autumn: ripe, luscious, ready, prepared, quickening and slowing. These are the decades of ripening and reaping *fruit*.

In our winter (the December, January, and February of life), we are the Muse, whose focus is on *inspiring* and whose symbol might be the *seed*. The inhale or ascent of the 70s is for *distilling* our knowledge, life, essence in order to exhale or descend into *empowering* ourselves and others through wisdom. These are the decades of becoming the essence of the *seed*. The song of the Muse is the song of winter: stark, quietude, inward, dreaming, potent, humble. Ideally, the cold and dark of the bared and pristine winter allow us to prepare for restoring ourselves to our original source and humanity to greater good.

The "flighty" emotionality of the Maiden and Maker becomes "grounded" during the Maven and Muse years. And, the primary task required in order to complete the transition from Maven to Muse is that of integration. New connections between our brain hemispheres during our fifties invite us to integrate our logical and relational thinking modes. We have the opportunity as well to integrate the lessons of the transitions from Maiden to Maker and Maker to Maven with the transition from Maven to Muse.

Are you finding, perhaps, that you are learning to integrate the personal with the professional (at last!) and the professional with the personal as you reenter a focus on that sphere of life? We might choose to integrate the personal with the political as well. We may also mature spiritually to integrate aversion to suffering with love and compassion for all experience.

Every time we move from one stage of life to another, we are recreating our self through a death and rebirth; and even that process itself involves a set of stages. In *Mother-Daughter Wisdom*, Dr. Christiane Northrup says,

> …every significant creation in our lives, whether it be a child, a work of art, a home, a relationship, or our life itself, requires an investment of life energy similar to that of a human pregnancy…. Each creation also requires a support structure to sustain and nourish it, just as the human placenta nourishes the unborn child…. [E]ach of our creations goes through essentially the same stages that women go through when we create and birth new life into the world. The biological and cosmic processes of conception, pregnancy, labor, birth, and the postpartum period are physical metaphors for how we create everything in our lives (25).

In fact, the growth cycle represented by the four stages is a series of birthings. The Maiden gives birth to the Maker, and the Maiden and Maker give birth to the Maven. The fulfillment of all three stages is required to give birth to the Muse. Consider how your childhood was the mother of your young adult self and then how your Maker and Maiden combined gave rise to the Maven you may now be. Consider how necessary it is for the first three stages to be fulfilled before you can birth your Muse. Perhaps for the first time, you will now be able to consciously and deliberately procreate your own fourth season of life. How would you like to begin that process?

The fulfillment of each stage is not only necessary to give rise to the next, but once experienced, every stage remains available to us. Just as there are spring-like days in winter or wintry days in summer, the seasons of our life also offer forays into sensations or experiences of youth or agedness. Much like the remnant of the tender sapling always present within a growing tree, our Maiden energy remains within to be summoned in moments of youthful joy, when at play with babies and young children, or when an infusion of joy is required to brighten some dark time. For me, every summer calls forth my Maker as I find myself energized to restore my outer environs, plant, water, and tend daily—well past the evening hour when in winter I find myself feeling tired. How do you notice your Maiden and Maker manifesting in your life?

Sometimes we can and must draw upon the latent skills of a stage yet to be fully experienced. How many of us, when confronted with some looming challenge find ourselves rising to it with a presence and wisdom beyond our years? Can you think of difficult times when you were a Maiden or Maker that you met with the maturity of a Maven or Muse? Whatever our life course, as women, we are likely to experience many of the same urges, desires, and life events whenever they happen to occur chronologically in our unique life span.

Taken both as stages of development and as recurring archetypes that manifest throughout our lives, the songs of the four stages blend together to create the harmony of a woman's life. And, just as we began this book together in a conversation over tea, you can invite these aspects of yourself to join you for a tea party any time you wish to conjure their energy and wisdom. Can you imagine conversing with your own inner wisdom personified by your Maiden, Maker, Maven, and Muse?

As we seek our own essence and the meaning of our career to our life, we will not only be integrating our clarified experiences into our own future, but also into the futures of younger women and our profession. What untold satisfactions have yet to arise from such an endeavor? What a time of our life is yet to come!

The time of your life

The good old days are now. *Tom Clancy*

We come to the fullness of time by adjusting our perspective and by living—and aging—in the now. We can do this by realizing that eternity is not a quantity of time but rather a quality of time. *Marita Grudzen and James P. Oberle*

Life is a succession of moments. To live each one is to succeed. *Corita Kent*

Every moment is a golden one for him who has the vision to recognize it as such. *Henry Miller*

If we don't change, we don't grow. If we don't grow, we aren't really living. *Gail Sheehy*

When I dare to be powerful, to use my strength in the service of my vision, then it becomes less and less important whether I am afraid. *Audre Lorde*

When we learn to say a deep, passionate yes to the things that really matter, then peace begins to settle onto our lives like golden sunlight sifting to a forest floor. *Thomas Kinkade*

The imperative was to shift from creating for a purpose to creating for the joy and challenge of the undertaking. *Sara Davidson*

One of the disciplines of building a rich soul life seems to be the simple act, on a daily basis, of remembering what is most important to us. *David Whyte*

Something is gained with schedules, but much is lost. The natural flow of life is broken into units and managed rather than experienced. *Mary Pipher*

[We] are starved for 'more' time, but the more time we…get, the more time we 'save,' the hungrier we become, the less we actually live. And…it is not exactly more time, more days and years, that we are starved for, it is *the present moment*. Through our increasing absorption in busyness, we have lost the present moment. 'Right away' is not *now*. *Jacob Needleman* (10)

The position of the sun, the stars, the seasons, the ebb and flow of nature undergirded early time reckoning, and each worked perfectly well under the circumstances. Time was relational, not absolute, geared to the flux of proximal circumstances and widely regarded as natural or God given. *Jon Hendricks*

[M]en are more closely bound to a kind of linear clock time than are women, who experience what may be characterized by cyclical or at least not as rigidly linear time and thereby age-grading. If that is indeed the case, it allows for more than a bit of ambiguity in terms of personal definitions of age. *Jon Hendricks*

I have long been fascinated and inspired by the roles and relationships of the two hemispheres in our amazing brains. So, I was thrilled to learn that one mark of maturity, recently identified in scientific studies, is enhanced integration between the hemispheres of the brain and therefore the two thinking modes—the left or logical and the right or relational. Some studies point to increased communication between the hemispheres as a compensatory adaptation for decreased brain cell growth as we age. For many in mid-life, this development is distinguished by increased access to and satisfaction from the more wholistic, creative, relational mode. The resurgence of right-brain dominance also alters our personal perception of time.

How fascinating that the functioning of the dual brain modes intersects with the perception and experience of time! According to Bob Samples in *The Metaphoric Mind*, the "dominant time mode of natural systems is cyclic. The dominant time mode of our culture is linear. Humankind preferred cyclic time until about 10,000 years ago. Humankind (at least the dominant cultures on earth) now prefers linear time" (37). He attributes this to the cultural dominance of rational, logical or left-mode thinking over wholistic, metaphorical or right-mode thinking, and he claims, "…the left cerebral hemisphere is specialized to process linear time. The right hemisphere is specialized to house an awareness of the cyclical" (33).

Young children are essentially relational beings. The logical mode, far less developed at birth than the relational, generally becomes activated around the time baby teeth begin making way for the adult set. Anyone who has spent extended periods of time caring for preschoolers knows the divergence from workday contexts of time and rhythm. The world of the young child is oriented not to clocks or calendars, but to the needs of the body and short-term interest in immediate surroundings. Have you experienced a similar orientation on vacations, during extended periods of illness or hospitalization, or on occasions of birth or death?

Even if you have found your working life satisfying and enriching, you have probably chafed under imposed demands and an artificial relationship to time. As jobholders, career women, professionals, and contributors to society, we are inculcated with predetermined expectations, standards, mores, and values on each ring of that circle. It is difficult to separate out inclinations and preferences that may be more consistent with our unique worldview and personal needs and desires. Who am *I* really, we may well ask, based on my own heart and inner cadences, my own knowing and sense of rightness?

Most of us experience a deep, knowing, inner voice or awareness that has accompanied us throughout life. As we mature, we are more inclined to pay attention to that felt sense and perhaps even to seek it out or deliberately become open to its presence and promptings. Some call this the inner mind, higher self, transcendent spirit, or, simply, soul. We know it as true, abiding, and comforting. Come The Autumn of life, you may, finally, hear clearly the song of your own soul and choose to harmonize your life to its melody.

How does your soul sing to you? Do you hear it in dreams, insights, images, desires, promptings, or "visions"? Under what conditions has your inner being come through most clearly or often? Can you identify a time of day or time of year? Is it when you are still or active, alone or with others? Does it sing as you walk, run, swim, dance, play a musical instrument, or sing yourself? Do you hear it when you are creating something, gardening, or cooking? Have you developed a practice of prayer or meditation?

In *The Five Stages of the Soul*, Harry R. Moody and David Carroll identify a spiraling loop that typifies urges toward the soul: the call, the search, the struggle, the breakthrough, the return. Have you been noticing an inner restlessness and questioning? Do you feel called to reconsider your priorities? Have you been looking for new and different ways to do things or to be? When you contemplate change, do you notice an inner push and pull—the desire for an 'else' accompanied by a fear of losing what is known and secure? Have you experienced how the excitement of the new always subsides, and what was once a dramatic change becomes familiar? All of us have experienced those five stages, sometimes in isolation, sometimes in a sequence, and sometimes in a redundant jumble.

Are you feeling urged from within to listen more closely to your soul? As you consider your priorities for a new career or a time of life that is likely to be more self-determined than any other, you may wish to create a time of retreat for yourself in which you have the time and space to notice if your soul is calling to you, or if you are experiencing any other stage in the round of spiritual development. Following a long-term career, you will likely require a period of readjustment and reorientation to rediscover a comfort zone with less structured action. A retreat is an opportunity to allow your own natural rhythms and inner world to ascend and dominate. When you have provided such respite for yourself in the past, how and why did the more relaxed rhythms differ from the rhythms and awareness of your working world?

As career women many of us have felt compelled to "do it all"—the career along with home, relationships, interests, causes, vacations, etc., etc. We are multitask masters, but slaves to the clock, the calendar, the schedule, and relentless, endless to-do lists. Our routines and then our very lives get folded into rigid compartments with little regard for the natural flow of days or cycles of seasons, let alone our biorhythms, stages of development, or markers of time. The tasks go on regardless of time of day or night, weather extremes, health issues, crises, or the cries of children or the planet.

Motivation, goal-setting, planning, determination, and persistence have been the ticket to "success" for many of us. In fact, planning has become a hallmark of our culture—sometimes beginning with kindergarten. Our education is planned; we plan for our careers, weddings, children, holiday celebrations, leisure time, vacations, and, of course, retirement. The "future" has become a specific, mapped-out *place* that we march to armed with goals, objectives, a plan, and clear expectations. Consider the sense of control that advance planning and preparations have provided you. Consider as well the disappointments, frustrations, and dissatisfaction that you have experienced as a result of thwarted expectations.

Rather than planning another future folded into goals and expectations, consider just looking ahead, outwardly and inwardly, with a soft, inclusive gaze while holding a sense of possibility and expectancy. When you look to the future with expectancy rather than predetermined expectations, you can remain open to the unfolding without annoyance, disappointment, frustration, or dissatisfaction. In fact, you can embrace appreciation for what is and enormous satisfaction with the unfolding. Certainly Mother Nature prefers to proceed in fits and starts, often declining the logical or anticipated progression, to provide instead the late or early frost, the unseasonable weather, even the natural disaster.

As professionals, we have been "in the know." However, to paraphrase Shunryu Suzuki, in the expert's mind, there are few possibilities, but "in the beginner's mind there are many." As career women in an autumn or The Autumn of life, we can embrace the joy of not knowing—the play of the novice mind, the openness of the unfolding being. After seasons of making something of your self and establishing an identity, perhaps you are ready to allow yourself to just *be*—not even who or what or how or why—yourself, *just* yourself—a letting go, an unfolding…

> If your mind is empty it is always ready for anything; it is open to everything. In the beginner's mind there are many possibilities; in the expert's mind there are few. *Shunryu Suzuki*

experience your life stages imaginatively

Imagine SPRING! The first stirrings are underground in the warming moist soil where roots awaken to stretch, reach, extend. Just as the very first task of a seed opening in the soil is to take root, the first stage of a child's life is establishing the roots of her being through mother, family, home, play, and school. Imagine the bud of childhood ripening, and the young girl frolicking like a colt, along a gurgling brook. What are some of the icons of girlhood? A wildflower garland, a fairy wand, dolls and dollhouses, pink dresses and stained overalls, a heart locket, ballet slippers, birthday cakes and surprises… What are the images that arise for you as you recall your own girlhood?

Adolescence brings a deepening as the bud blossoms into the teen maiden. Roots continue to deepen as the sapling reaches upward and outward. The teenage girl begins to cultivate her wings with her first experiences of love and betrayal, triumph and failure, dreams and disappointments. The treasures of the Maiden are preserved in diaries, memory books, boxes, and closets: first dance, first date, first kiss, first love, first job, new relationships, accomplishments, graduations… What memories of your teen years are preserved in your heart?

Imagine SUMMER! Like burgeoning plant life and rushing river, the 20-something's awareness of inner growth stimulates new yearning and extended reaching… a celebration of ascendant growth, development, striving, and gaining—so much promise, so much to do and be and get and have! So many hats to wear! The focus is on branching out—new friends and lovers, activities and experiences. We know now that, unlike males who are driven by fight or flight, females are prompted by tending and befriending. These urges blossom during the decades of the Maker. The young woman in her 20s and 30s is not only the home maker, but is also branching out to make her career, perhaps a name for herself; to make a variety of relationships, perhaps a marriage and family; and to make her way in life, and shape an expanded sense of self.

In what ways did you branch out, extending and shaping yourself, when you were a Maker in your 20s and 30s? The intense excitement of these years is often tempered by anxieties and concerns. If you could return to yourself at that time and whisper reassurances into your own younger ear, how would you comfort yourself?

Imagine AUTUMN! Subtle changes are signaled by the angle and quality of light and by deepening colors reflected in a flowing stream. The bounty of the season is prime for harvesting. The colors and fragrances of fruits are intoxicating. Then, nature's gradual lessening gives way to preparing. Trees scatter transformed leaves; release seeds to perpetuity; slow rich, amber sap, and stabilize growth. In her 40s and 50s, the Maven is about fulfilling. She spends her 40s rising to the top of her game, and the deepening of her 50s manifests in the power of reigning. She becomes the Queen Mother…. Inner knowing transcends imposed values, and perspective shifts and becomes more personal even as it expands. She finds herself reflected in those who preceded her journey as well as in those who will follow hers. The Maven is mindful of legacies fulfilled and those yet to be realized. This is a richly satisfying and evocative time. What has been the path of your own ascent into the autumn of life? As Maven, how will you choose to reap the harvest and deepen the bounty?

Imagine WINTER! The bracing cold, icy winds, sustaining rain, and pristine snows prompt retreat—retreat into less busyness, greater stillness, deeper inner knowing, quiet time for the soul. Trees stand proudly against the stark sky, their form revealed, essence exposed—a proud new silhouette, imperious presence reclaimed. Like the tree, the latter decades of the Muse are a time to shed all pretense and liberate the crone. Now you can recreate her image in your own inner beauty, perhaps incorporating the concepts of humor and contemplation that are derived from the root word muse. You can also recreate any aversion to the increased darkness of winter by considering it as a time of preparation for restoring your being…to original source…and for inspiring *all* to greater good.

Icons of the Muse include the cleansing broom, placid pool, soothing tea, transmuting mortar and pestle, powerful distilled infusions, candles and illumination… What icons would you add to this list?

That which remains of your essence beyond your physical being are seeds. Think about the mysterious potential of seeds. What seeds will you prepare in your winter of life?

Savor the images and insights of this inner journey through the four seasons of a woman's life.

Acorns

Who have I become through my work?

What has my work become through me?

Who am I now becoming?

How will I cultivate who I am now becoming?

Having read this chapter, what particularly stimulates or energizes you?

What holds the most value for you?

What deliberate process(es) are you inspired to create?

What spontaneous process(es) do you expect you will have the opportunity to allow?

If you underlined, doodled, or journaled as you read this chapter, review that now and notice:

Any meaning evident now that was not apparent as you wrote or drew.

Anything that surprises or particularly pleases you.

Any redundancies or patterns.

Anything you wish to complete or follow up with.

Go through this chapter again and respond to the in-text questions. Notice anywhere you feel uncertain, incomplete, intrigued, or pulled, which may provide important clues about how you have yet to fulfill your career…

How do you wish to benefit from this chapter?

Return to these questions in the future to notice any changes in your responses.

Stepping Stones

There is a song to every stage of a woman's life that carries the melody of the corresponding season. Taken together the songs of the seasons create the harmony of a woman's life cycle.

Narrative Journaling Experiences

List defining events, experiences, choices of your career and/or life. Group them together thematically. Select one or more of the groupings to write about.

What do you cherish most about your Maiden and when does she arise in your life?

What was one of the best things you learned as a Maker and how do you apply that now?

Over what facets of your life do you now "reign," and for what particular qualities would you crown your Maven self?

What will you "brew" as a Muse, and how will your Muse honor the three personas that have evolved into her?

Visual Journaling Experiences

Create a chart in which you divide your life by seven-year periods or by decades vertically down the page. The seven-year periods can each represent a month of the year: 0-6 = January, 7-13 = February, 14-20 = March, 21-27 = April, 29-34 = May, 35-41 = June, 42-48 = July, 49-55 = Aug, 56-62 = September, 63-69 = October, 70-76 = November, 77- = December. Or, the decades can represent seasons: 0-10, 11-20 = spring (March-May); 21-30, 31-40, 41-50 = summer (June-August); 51-60, 61-70 = autumn (September-November); 71- = winter (December-February). Create three horizontal columns—Challenges, Gifts, Legacies—and complete them for each time period. Create a second chart for your seven-year periods or decades yet to come, with columns for Possible Futures, Heart Callings, Overlay. After filling in the first two columns, look for where they are the same and complete the third.

Spectrums: Create a series of spectrums and place yourself where you believe you are now and where you would like to be. Use images to represent each pole of the spectrum. For example:

Old - New
Aged - Ageless
Box - Sphere
Small Part - Big Picture
Bifurcated - Integrated
Compartmentalized - Wholistic
Closed - Open
Safe - Exploring
Stuck - Creative
Outer Determined - Inner Determined
Follower - Pioneer
Critical - Appreciative
Ego - Authentic Self
Status Quo - Heart Callings

Visually represent each season of the year. Record notable springs, summers, autumns, and winters of your life on the appropriate visual representations. You are probably familiar with the Biblical verse from Ecclesiastes III or the 1952 Pete Seeger song "Turn!, Turn!, Turn!," which declare that "To every thing there is a season, and a time to every purpose under the heaven…a time to be born, and a time to die; a time to plant, and a time to pluck up that which is planted… a time to break down, and a time to build up…a time to mourn, and a time to dance…a time to cast away stones, and a time to gather stones together…a time to get, and a time to lose; a time to keep, and a time to cast away…." What was the "time for" provided by each of your notable seasons?

Create a visual representation for the persona of each stage of a woman's life: Maiden, Maker, Maven, Muse. Be creative! Create a collage for each, a paper doll, an oversized card (as if part of a "deck"), or a sculpture, painting, drawing, poster. Dress four dolls or figurines or stuffed animals to represent the stages. You might incorporate one or more themes, e.g., a collage or drawing of hats or shoes for each stage, or represent each season visually. Reflect on each representation and allow them to interact among each other. Pose questions that each answers. Ask each to pose questions to the others. Ask each to predict your future or to reflect upon your past. Engage them in a conversation. Ask them to describe your next season of life.

Create a mandala representing the four life stages. One easy way to do this is to use a paper plate and draw intersecting vertical and horizontal lines, creating four "slices." Draw, paint, color, or collage each section to represent the Maiden, Maker, Maven, and Muse. Consider the presence of all of them at every life stage. Under what circumstances might you call upon each of them? When might each of them arise spontaneously from within you?

Interpersonal Experiences
Share with someone each of your selves at each of your four stages. Project how you might be as Maven or Muse if you are not there yet.

Invite one or more women friends to explore together the four stages of a woman's life through conversation or a more playful medium, such as a collage or skit.

continuing

YOUR JOURNEY

musings

ON CYCLING AND RECYCLING THRU TIME

…growth spirals, sometimes quite slowly, yet always lifting me beyond where I've been.
Rosalie Deer Heart and Alison Strickland (150)

Our way of knowing is the very thing that constrains our knowledge. Our systems of understanding are the constructions that enable us to have knowledge, but they also set limits beyond which we cannot know, like the horizon on the ocean, an invisible barrier to a world unseen. Human perceptions, no matter how powerful, elegant, and self-consistent, are bounded and this bounds us.
John Broomfield (162)

How is one to live a moral and compassionate existence when one is fully aware of the blood, the horror inherent in life, when one finds darkness not only in one's culture but within oneself? If there is a stage at which an individual life becomes truly adult, it must be when one grasps the irony in its unfolding and accepts responsibility for a life lived in the midst of such paradox. One must live in the middle of contradiction, because if all contradiction were eliminated at once life would collapse. There are simply no answers to some of the great pressing questions. You continue to live them out, making your life a worthy expression of leaning into the light. *Barry Lopez*

There is vitality, a life force, an energy, a quickening that is translated through you into action, and because there is only one of you in all time, this expression is unique…You have to keep open and aware directly to the urges that motivate you. Keep the channel open… [There is] no satisfaction whatever at any time. There is only a queer, divine dissatisfaction, a blessed unrest that keeps us marching and makes us more alive than the other. *Martha Graham*

My second floor bedroom window faces the eastern sky. When roused by the summer sun, I luxuriate for a bit in the diffuse green of apple tree leaves—almost as if abed in a tree house. When I awake in winter, I gaze through the patterns of branches sharply delineated by a brightening sky. Whatever the season, eventually my soft gaze becomes focused to observe the multi-colored wind catcher suspended just outside the window. It is a narrow helix of rainbow hues descending from violet to red. Weighted with a small red wooden sphere, it spins with the slightest movement of air.

I am always mesmerized by the illusions of colors bleeding one into the other or circulating upwards or downwards. Although I know, of course, what is "really" occurring, I remain delighted and mystified by the perception that inspires me to drowsily spin metaphors and analogies. Oh, how life cycles and shifts and returns…

Just beyond the apple tree, a weather vane arrow tops a neighborhood gazebo. I do not care to draw my life with that form. It is so pointed, so finite, so intent on a single direction… "Taken as an upward piling of years, shooting (faster and faster it seems) along the number line, the birthday count is a vector with a rate and a direction—an arrow," says Tyler Volk in *Metapatterns* (165). The arrow, of course, points to "death," and, as we are so bounded by our fear of that irrevocable conclusion, we rarely even use the word without hushed tones. Our aversion to a higher birthday count and the process of aging arises from that dread of the end, of time running out. And as David Whyte notes, "Without an appreciation of the hours of life, we are simply a target for our own incoming death…." (173). However, one's lifeline need not be perceived as a straight trajectory. It would, in fact, be more natural, and certainly more satisfying, to project it as a spiral—ever cycling. Volk notes, "Cycles are the heartbeats of understanding. A thing perceived is just an event. Repeated it opens up to the instruments of science, the examinations of philosophers, the imaginations of shamans" (233).

What is your current relationship with cycles, with "the hours of life"—time? Do you ever have enough time? Is it ever on your side or are you always running short of it? As you cycle into or through an autumn season of life, is your quality of time or a felt lack of time to do what you most desire a primary motivator of your readiness for change? Is it your expectation that different, less, or no 'work' will mean better or more time? Do you expect to experience time differently if you make changes in your career status? Will your experiences in an autumn of life comprise a new cycle or stage in the time of your life?

Our Western constructs for moving through the cycles and seasons of life are dominated by left-brain thinking, i.e., focused, logical, analytical, linear, sequential, literal, calculating, and critical. Women in general, however, and especially menopausal and postmenopausal women as it turns out, are more inclined towards integrated or right-mode experiences. Physically, we embody explicit life cycles and "mother" nature through our emotions, hormones, menses, pregnancy, birthing, and care taking—whether specific functions are experienced literally or figuratively. These physical and metaphorical experiences reinforce our relationships to our bodies, feelings, others, environments, flora and fauna, time, and even planetary influences.

Etymologically, the Western European concept of time (and it is, of course very different in many other cultures) was derived from awareness of the tide. "Tide" is defined by the *Online Etymology Dictionary* as "point or portion of time, due time," "division of time. Meaning 'rise and fall of the sea' (1340) is probably via notion of 'fixed time,' specifically 'time of high water'" [tide. Dictionary.com. Online Etymology Dictionary. Douglas Harper, Historian. http://dictionary.reference.com/browse/tide (accessed: February 27, 2007)]. *Dictionary.com* defines tide as "anything that alternately rises and falls, increases and decreases, etc.: the tide of the seasons" [tide. Dictionary.com. Dictionary.com Unabridged (v 1.1). Random House, Inc. http://dictionary.reference.com/browse/tide (accessed: February 27, 2007)].

Over time, however, the notion of time became instrumentalized, codified, rigidified. Since Western civilization found it impossible to make the natural flow of the universe fit into our tidy measurements, we developed adjustments to keep it on track—including the leap year and annual adjustments to the atomic clock. We sought to constrain time and bind it with the very instruments we devised to observe and measure it. Most concepts of age and aging, of one's life as taking its "course" (as though such a passage can be predefined, predetermined), are derived from such a bounded notion of time.

The tides, which may have suggested the notion of "fixed time," are more profound in what they demonstrate of varying intervals that beat out a pulse, cadence, rhythm, and cycles. Our breath is the rhythm of the ocean, the rhythm of life, the rhythm of cycles. The inhale is followed by the exhale, expansion by contraction, organization by dissipation, day by night, summer by fall. If you are pressed for and by time, you may find it useful to notice that time is not growing shorter, running out, or passing away—it is cycling.

The spiral is a free-form life metaphor. Are the colors of the wind catcher circulating upwards or downwards? It is irrelevant—for both ascendancy and descendancy complete the form, complement and enable each other, support and allow each other. We can value resolution and dissolution, breakthrough and breakdown, epiphany and despair, clarity and confusion, energy and enervation, harmony and dissonance, transcendence and dissipation…because no yin is possible without its yang.

Once we accept that oscillation is mandatory, we can notice the choices we have about the patterns, intervals, heights, and depths of our own cycles.

Although a lengthening past presents a continuum, a backwards glance offers a view of our own rippling wake that is probably not a simple straight line. From ahead the perspective may reveal predictable patterns and continuing cycles of growth and development. As maturing adults we probably feel that we know our self, what characterizes our personality, "who we are." We may be able to smile knowingly when we catch our selves doing what we usually do in response to a situation. We know our preferences, inclinations, tendencies, typical responses and behaviors, our personal norms and conventions, our established pathways. We can examine the observable cycles of our past through the science of psychology, the art of an applied philosophy, or our own inner knowing, to paraphrase Volk.

Contemporary interest in human potential seems to focus on our attraction to the positive, the heights, the gains, the peak experiences. And, indeed, that which uplifts is rich and satisfying. When life is perceived as cycling, however, descendant motion is experienced as enabling depth, balance and the return to ascendancy. Angeles Arrien claims, "Each descent prepares us for the ascent, the magnificent climb that integrates more of our essential being" (15). We don't hold our breath because it feels good to be filled, we exhale in order to release, refresh, and, of course, refill. Human growth cycles in a spiral form. Once beyond the amazing growth of the young child, we experience little that is completely new—most experiences offer an opportunity to RE-new.

As you consider the pulsations and oscillations of life through time, where in the cycles of ascent and descent are the fulfilling and shifting of your career? Are you uplifted, energized, filled with anticipation—on the ascent? Are you reluctant, concerned, anxious—riding a descent? If you sense ebbing, acknowledge that it will give rise to flow. When you notice waning, remain open to the inevitable waxing. Remember that each position is appropriate and likely, and that each direction actually leads to the other. The ascent requires momentum, and the descent can stimulate exhilaration. In fact, because it is the ever-shifting tension between the oscillations that creates momentum, creativity, movement, and change, we are well served to fully experience each swing of the pendulum as well as the brief moment of suspension between them.

We all self-regulate, even if on an other-than-conscious level, our range and quotas of stress, challenge, pleasure, discomfort, exertion, and relaxation. With awareness of oscillations, we can experience transitions as unfoldings. One way to do this is by noticing the momentary pause between an inhale, expansion, or ascent and exhale, contraction, or descent. This almost imperceptible interlude allows the next natural arc of the spiral. It is a space for nothing and everything. You can enter into it to experience neutrality and create choice. It is the threshold between culmination and initiation.

We can go beyond the limits of time and allow cycles of time to both dwell within us—intrinsic, natural, and vital—and to project before us—always. As you consider the seasons and stages of your career and life, imagine each phase as an arc of your life's spiral. Notice how each arc includes a beginning, middle and end; builds on and includes the past as well as the future; creates movement from, to *and* within; and generates repetition both within and among cycles. Notice also the value of processing or composting between cycles. Your current autumn can provide the opportunity to pause on your own threshold between seasons.

in a group setting

One of the pleasures of cultivating this book was collaborating with Susan Anthes to develop and present workshops based on the themes, concepts, and activities. Susan and I piloted many of the Acorns and Stepping Stones with one small group of women during four evenings in spring 2007 and with another group during a one-day "retreat" in summer 2007.

I was a little skeptical about the effectiveness of covering so much material in a single day, but the results of the retreat day were very satisfying. I attribute this, at least in part, to our efforts at creating a retreat environment—a relaxing setting, wonderful shared food, and the mutual intention to make it a focused, valuable, and special day.

The group environment is a very stimulating and inspiring way to experience the book.

Your own shared experiences are witnessed and affirmed, and you have the benefit of broadening your perspective as you listen to the shared experiences of the others. We certainly found the groups uplifting and empowering. And, I'd like to acknowledge here my appreciation to the wonderful women who joined us in our groups!

The most consistent feedback we received from participants in both groups was how powerful the questions were for them. In fact, I received the same feedback from the women who were early manuscript readers.

The outlines that follow are mere skeletons to stimulate your own thinking. Each is followed by some suggestions for variation. Better yet, be creative and have fun making the material work for you and your friends!

Harvest the Bounty of Your Career One-Day Retreat
9 a.m.-5:30 p.m.

Convener provides:
Set of four handouts for each participant (see below)
Magazines for tearing out images
Scissors, glue sticks and/or double-sided tape (or participants can be asked to bring their own)

Participants bring:
Notebook and/or journal
Pen or set of fine-point colored markers
Piece of cardboard (at least 8 ½ x 11" or larger)
Optional: Images for collage

Handouts: Each of the following question sets should appear at the top of a page with blank space below for writing.

1.
What roots have I grown as a result of my career?
What roots have I contributed to my workplace?
In what ways has my career provided a root system for my life?
What nourishes my roots and all that arises from them?
What will I harvest from my roots and cultivate in the next arc of my life spiral?

2.
What branches have I grown during my career/life?
In what ways has my career/life branched out?
In what ways would I like to branch out now?
In what ways has my career provided a social system for my life—e.g., professional and social
    contacts, social activities during and outside of work time, holiday or seasonal events…?

In what ways have I extended myself and been shaped through my working relationships?

What will I harvest from my branches and cultivate in the next arc of my life spiral?

3.

What are the fruits of my career?

How have my fruits enhanced my workplace or my profession?

What are the fruits of my workplace?

Are the fruits of my career also the fruits of my life?

Do the fruits of my career, workplace, and life relate or intersect?

Would I perceive a lack in my life without the fruits of my career?

What will I harvest of my fruits and cultivate in the next arc of my life spiral?

4.

What has my career seeded in me?

What have I seeded in my workplace or profession?

In my career, what feels incomplete or seems to hold room for growth or development?

What new skills would I like to bring to the job?

In the next arc of my life, what do I want to bring, give, receive?

As I consider the patterns of my life and career and a possible new stage:

    What can I anticipate?

    What do I choose to nourish?

    What do I intend to receive?

    What will I offer?

    What will I harvest from my seeds and cultivate in the next arc of my life spiral?

A possible schedule:

9-10 a.m.

Personal Introductions. Each participant answers: Where do you see yourself in your life cycle?

Convener reads "Experience Your Life Stages Imaginatively" (page 143).

Group discussion of a woman's life cycle and four stages and what a career means in that context.

10-11 a.m.

A participant reads "Experience Roots Imaginatively" (page 46).

For the next 40 minutes, each participant starts a collage with some images representing her roots and responds to the first question set directly on the handout or in her journal.

Participants share for the last 15 minutes of the hour.

11 a.m.-12 p.m.

A participant reads "Experience Branches Imaginatively" (page 64).

For the next 40 minutes, each participant adds to her collage some images representing her branches and responds to the second question set directly on the handout or in her journal.

Participants share for the last 15 minutes of the hour.

12-12:30 p.m. Lunch

12:30-1:30 p.m.

A participant reads "Experience Fruits Imaginatively" (page 81).

For the next 40 minutes, each participant adds to her collage some images representing her fruits and responds to the third question set directly on the handout or in her journal.

Participants share for the last 15 minutes of the hour.

1:30-2:30 p.m.

A participant reads "Experience Seeds Imaginatively" (page 98).

For the next 40 minutes, each participant adds to her collage some images representing her seeds and responds to the fourth question set directly on the handout or in her journal.

Participants share for the last 15 minutes of the hour.

2:30-3 p.m. Break and individual time to review responses

3-4 p.m.

A participant reads "Experience Your Harvest Imaginatively" (page 121).

Participants fill in their collage with images representing their desired harvest.

4-5:15 p.m.

Each participant shares her collage and responds to the following questions:

Who have I become through my work?

What has my work become through me?

Who am I now becoming?

How will I cultivate who I am now becoming?

5:15-5:30 p.m.

Wrap up and closing circle

Some possible variations:

Read or create a handout of a selection of quotes provided throughout the book or excerpts that address some issues you know participants may be interested in.

Conduct all the discussions in the morning and use the afternoon to collage.

Instead of collaging roots, branches, fruits, and seeds, collage Maiden, Maker, Maven, Muse.

Substitute other activities for the collage, such as skits or another form of visual representation.

Ask the participants to read the book or selected sections for preparation (although the workshop can actually stand alone without advance reading).

Some considerations:

Group size

Location

Earlier or later start/end times

A longer lunch for more socializing

A potluck lunch or dinner afterwards

Two half-day sessions

Guidelines for a Series of Two-hour (or longer) Harvest Gatherings

Convener provides:

A set of quote cards for each session: Copy some of the quotes from each chapter onto individual index cards. At each session, participants select a card for the chapter to be covered and read the quote aloud to the group

Magazines for tearing out images

Scissors, glue sticks and/or double-sided tape (or participants can be asked to bring their own)

Participants bring:

Notebook and/or journal

Pen or set of fine-point colored markers

Piece of cardboard (at least 8 ½ x 11" or larger)

Optional: Images for collage

Basic format:

1. Each participant shares *briefly*.
2. Each participant reads aloud a quote card and says why the quote is significant for her.
3. Each participant shares whatever comes first to her mind about the day's theme.
4. In group discussion, participants respond to the question set to develop the theme (see sets for each theme below).
5. Participants divide into pairs to select and engage with an Interpersonal Experience from the book.
6. Group reconvenes and discusses Interpersonal Experiences.
7. A participant reads aloud the Imaginative Experience for the day's theme.
8. Participants work on their individual cumulative collages.
9. Group reconvenes and debriefs the day's theme.
10. Convener previews theme of next gathering.

Guidelines for Convener:

For each session create a timed schedule by determining the amount of time likely for each segment based on the number of participants.

Keep the group roughly on time for each piece and make adjustments as you go. Consider using a timer to keep the opening time for sharing limited to a *brief* update that does not become an extended monologue.

If participants are not able to gather for seven sessions, the most important chapters are Roots, Branches, Fruits, and Seeds. Elements of those chapters preceding Roots can be incorporated into the Roots gathering, and Your Harvest can be incorporated into Seeds.

The reading of the day's Imaginative Experience will transition participants into a more creative state of mind. Before the reading, be sure everyone is set up to begin collaging immediately after the reading without any disruption or discussion. Consider background music for collaging—music of the Baroque period (e.g., Vivaldi, Bach, Handle, Paganini, etc.) is especially conducive for creating a relaxed and creative state of mind.

Be flexible and creative! You can, for example, substitute another Visual Journaling Experience for the collage activity. The important thing is to provide time for engaging the creative side of the brain. The group itself may want to modify the suggested format.

Some considerations:

Group size

Location

Day of week/time of day

Refreshments

Concluding each session with a potluck

Question Sets by Chapter/Session/Theme

Four-Part Harmony of a Woman's Life Cycle

What do you cherish most about your Maiden and when does she arise in your life?

What was one of the best things you learned as a Maker and how do you apply that now?

Over what facets of your life do you now "reign," and for what particular qualities would you crown your Maven self?

What will you "brew" as a Muse, and how will your Muse honor the three personas that have evolved into her?

How has your career affected/determined your life stages—past, present, future?

The Bounty of a Career/To Harvest

How do you define "career"?

How different would your life be had you not dedicated the time and energy thus far in the development of one or more endeavors that you would describe as a career?

How different would your personal identity be without the context of a career?

To what extent has your life and your sense of self been shaped by a career?

What have been the rewards and sacrifices?

How will your current choices and your future be determined by your career?

Address the culmination of your career as your personal "bounty."

Roots

What roots have you grown as a result of your career?

What roots have you contributed to your workplace?

In what ways has your career provided a root system for your life?

What nourishes your roots and all that arises from them?

Branches

What branches have you grown during your career/life?

In what ways has your career/life branched out?

In what ways would you like to branch out now?

In what ways has your career provided a social system for your life—e.g., professional and social contacts, social activities during and outside of work time, holiday or seasonal events…?

In what ways have you extended yourself and been shaped through your working relationships?

Fruits

What are the fruits of your career?

How have your fruits enhanced your workplace?

What are the fruits of your workplace?

Are the fruits of your career also the fruits of your life?

Do the fruits of your career, workplace, and life relate or intersect?

Do you think you would perceive a lack in your life without the fruits of your career?

Seeds

What has your career seeded in you?

What have you seeded in your workplace?

In your career, what feels incomplete or seems to hold room for growth or development? What new skills would you like to bring to the job?

In the next arc of your life, what do you want to bring, give, and receive?

As you consider the patterns of your life and career and a possible new stage, ask yourself:

    What can I anticipate?

    What do I choose to nourish?

    What do I intend to receive?

    What will I offer?

Your Harvest

What will I now choose to harvest from my career for the next arc in the spiral of my life?

What else would I like to grow and harvest in my life?

As you consider the patterns of your life and career and a possible new stage, ask yourself:

> What can I anticipate?
>
> What do I choose to nourish?
>
> What do I intend to receive?
>
> What will I offer?

In the next arc of your life, what do you want to bring, give, and receive?

And/or

What do you like most about your collage?

What does it say about you, your career, your life?

What do you learn about yourself and your career?

What does it say to you—what suggestions or advice does it offer?

What next life intentions are manifest in it?

What does it suggest you do next?

What is most inspiring about your collage?

inspiration

A COLLECTION OF ADDITIONAL READING

As I mentioned in the first chapter, during my early fifties I finally faced my nagging concerns about aging by searching for the meaning and value of the second half of life and looking to nature and books for answers. This is the complete bibliography of books, articles, and websites I consulted prior to and while writing this book. The asterisked items are among the most inspirational to me and are my suggestions to you for more reading if you wish to continue your journey with additional books.

*Arrien, Angeles. *The Second Half of Life: Opening the Eight Gates of Wisdom*. Boulder, CO: Sounds True, 2005.

*Autry, James A. *The Spirit of Retirement: Creating a Life of Meaning and Personal Growth*. Roseville, CA: Prima, 2002.

*Baruss, Imants. *Authentic Knowing: The Convergence of Science and Spiritual Aspiration*. West Lafayette, IN: Purdue University Press, 1996.

*Borysenko, Joan. *A Woman's Book of Life: The Biology, Psychology, and Spirituality of the Feminine Life Cycle*. NYC: Riverhead Books, 1998.

*Brizendine, Louann. *The Female Brain*. NYC: Morgan Road Books, 2006.

*Broomfield, John. *Other Ways of Knowing: Recharting Our Future with Ageless Wisdom*. Rochester, VT: Inner Traditions, 1997.

Buzan, Tony and Barry Buzan. *The Mind Map Book: How to Use Radiant Thinking to Maximize Your Brain's Untapped Potential*. London: BBC Books, 1995.

Cameron, Julia. *The Artist's Way: A Spiritual Path to Higher Creativity*. NYC: Jeremy P. Tarcher/Perigree Books, 1992.

*Cantor, Dorothy. *What Do You Want To Do When You Grow Up? Starting the Next Chapter of Your Life*. Boston: Little, Brown, and Co., 2000.

Carter, Rita. *Mapping the Memory: Understanding Your Brain to Improve Your Memory*. Berkeley, CA: Ulysses Press, 2006.

*Cohen, Gene D. *The Creative Age: Awakening Human Potential in the Second Half of Life*. NYC: Avon, 2000.

*Cohen, Gene D. *The Mature Mind: The Positive Power of the Aging Brain*. NYC: Basic Books, 2005.

*Corbett, David with Richard Higgins. *Portfolio Life: The New Path to Work, Purpose, and Passion After 50*. San Francisco, CA: John Wiley, 2007.

Crandell, Susan. *Thinking About Tomorrow: Reinventing Yourself at Midlife*. NYC: Wellnes Central, 2007.

Davidson, Sara. *Leap! What Will We Do with the Rest of Our Lives: Reflections from the Boomer Generation*. NYC: Random House, 2008.

Deer Heart, Rosalie and Alison Strickland. *Harvesting Your Journals: Writing Tools to Enhance Your Growth and Creativity*. Santa Fe, NM: Heart Link Publications, 1999.

Dreher, Diane. *Inner Gardening: A Seasonal Path to Inner Peace*. NYC: Quill, 2002.

*Dreher, Diane. *Your Personal Renaissance: 12 Steps to Finding Your Life's True Calling*. Cambridge, MA: Da Capo Press, 2008.

*Dweck, Carol S. *Mindset: The New Psychology of Growth*. NYC: Random House, 2006.

Dychtwald, Ken and Daniel J. Kadlec. *The Power Years: A User's Guide to the Rest of Your Life*. NYC: Wiley, 2005.

*Erickson, Tamara. *Retire Retirement: Career Strategies for the Boomer Generation*. Boston, MA: Harvard Business Press, 2008.

Fischer, Kathleen. *Autumn Gospel: Women in the Second Half of Life*. Mahwah, NJ: Paulist Press, 1995.

*Freedman. Marc. *Encore: Finding Work That Matters in the Second Half of Life*. NYC: Public Affairs, 2007.

Friedan, Betty. *The Fountain of Age*. NYC: Simon and Schuster, 1993.

Frost, Nina H., Dr. Kenneth C. Ruge, and Dr. Richard W. Shoup. *Soul Mapping: An Imaginative Way to Self–Discovery*. NYC: Marlowe & Co., 2000.

Garofalo, Michael P. *Facts and Statistics for Gardeners*. http://www.gardendigest.com/facts.htm.

Goleman, Daniel. *Social Intelligence: The New Science of Human Relationships*. NYC: Bantam, 2006.

Greengard, Samuel. "Presto Change-O: It's no easy trick to switch careers at 50-plus, but more and more workers are taking the leap and starting over at jobs they love." *AARP Magazine*, Nov. & Dec. 2006, 77+.

Hageneder, Fred. *The Meaning of Trees: Botany, History, Healing, Lore*. San Francisco, CA: Chronicle Books, 2005.

Hageneder, Fred. *The Spirit of Trees: Science, Symbiosis, and Inspiration*. NYC: Continuum International, 2001.

*Harkness, Helen. *Capitalizing on Career Chaos: Bringing Creativity and Purpose to Your Work and Life*. Mountain View, CA: Davies-Black, 2005.

*Harkness, Helen. *Don't Stop the Career Clock: Rejecting the Myths of Aging for a New Way to Work in the 21st Century*. Palo Alto, CA: Davies-Black, 1999.

*Harris, Maria. *Jubilee Time: Celebrating Women, Spirit, and the Advent of Age*. NYC: Bantam, 1995.

Hayes, Charles D. *The Rapture of Maturity: A Legacy of Lifelong Learning*. Wasilla, AR: Autodidactic Press, 2004.

Heath, Jennifer, ed. *Uncontained: Writers and Photographers in the Garden and the Margins*. Boulder, CO: Baksun Books, 2007.

Hollis, James. *Finding Meaning in the Second Half of Llife: How to Finally, Really Grow Up*. NYC: Gotham, 2005.

Langer, Ellen J. *Mindfulness*. Reading, MA: Addison-Wesley, 1989.

Laney, Marti Olsen. *The Introvert Advantage: How to Thrive in an Extrovert World*. NYC: Workman, 2002.

*Levine, Suzanne Braun. *Inventing the Rest of Our Lives: Women in Second Adulthood*. NYC: Viking, 2005.

McFadden, Susan H. and Robert C. Atchley, eds. *Aging and the Meaning of Time*. NYC: Springer, 2001.

*McKenna, Elizabeth Perle. *When Work Doesn't Work Anymore: Women, Work, and Identity*. NYC: Delacorte Press, 1997.

Metcalf, Linda Trichter and Torin Simon. *Writing the Mind Alive: The Proprioceptive Method for Finding Your Authentic Voice*. NYC: Ballantine, 2002.

Moody, Harry R. and David L. Carroll. *The Five Stages of the Soul: Charting the Spiritual Passages That Shape Our Lives*. NYC: Anchor Books Doubleday, 1997.

Myss, Caroline. *Sacred Contracts: Awakening Your Divine Potential*. NYC: Harmony Books, 2001.

*Needleman, Jacob. *Time and the Soul: Where Has All the Meaningful Time Gone—And Can We Get It Back?* San Francisco, CA: Barrett-Koehler, 2003.

*Newman, Betsy Kyte. *Retiring as a Career: Making the Most of Your Retirement.* Westport, CT: Praeger, 2003.

Northrup, M.D., Christiane. *Mother-Daughter Wisdom: Creating a Legacy of Physical and Emotional Health.* NYC: Bantam, 2005.

Paterson, Jacqueline Memory. *Tree Wisdom.* London: Hammersmith, 1996.

Pearce, Joseph Chilton. *Magical Child: Rediscovering Nature's Plan for Our Children.* NYC: Bantam, 1986.

*Pollard, Dave. *Finding the Sweet Spot: The Natural Entrepreneur's Guide to Responsible, Sustainable, Joyful Work.* New River Junction, VT: Chelsea Green, 2008.

Rico, Gabriele Lusser. *Writing the Natural Way: Using Right-Brain Techniques to Release Your Expressive Powers.* Los Angeles, CA: Tarcher, 1983.

Richardson, Cheryl. "Create a Life Map." http://www.oprah.com/article/spirit/ss_know_passion_01/1.

Roman, Jorge H. and A. Shelly Spearing, "Knowledge Management," NIRMA/SCIENTECH Conference, 2005 Procedures and Nuclear Information Management Conference, 28-31 August 2005.

*Roszak, Theodore. *Longevity Revolution: As Boomers Become Elders.* Berkeley, CA: Berkeley Hills Books, 2001.

*Sadler, William A. and James H. Krefft. *Changing Course: Navigating Life after Fifty*. Centennial, CO: Center for Third Age Leadership Press, 2007.

*Samples, Bob. *The Metaphoric Mind: A Celebration of Creative Consciousness*, 2nd ed. Rolling Hills Estates, CA: Jalmar Press, 1993.

Savishinsky, Joel S. *Breaking the Watch: The Meanings of Retirement in America*. Ithaca, NY: Cornell University Press, 2000.

*Schachter-Shalomi, Zalman and Ronald S. Miller. *From Age-ing to Sage-ing: A Profound New Vision of Growing Older*. NYC: Warner, 1997.

*Sedlar, Jeri and Rick Miners. *Don't Retire, REWIRE! 5 Steps to Fulfilling Work That Fuels Your Passion, Suits Your Personality, or Fills Your Pocket*. Indianapolis, IN: Alpha Books, 2003.

Seligman, Martin E. P. *Authentic Happiness: Using the New Positive Psychology to Realize Your Potential for Lasting Fulfillment*. NYC: Free Press, 2002.

*Schlossberg, Nancy K. *Retire Smart. Retire Happy: Finding Your True Path in Life*. Washington, DC: American Psychological Assoc., 2004.

Sheehy, Gail. *New Passages: Mapping Your Life Across Time*. NYC: Random House, 1995.

*Sorin, Fran. *Digging Deep: Unearthing Your Creative Roots Through Gardening*. NYC: Warner, 2004.

Stone, Judith. "Meeting of the Minds: Interview of Daniel Goleman." *O: the Oprah Magazine*, Oct. 2006, 251-256.

Sullivan, Erin. *Saturn in Transit: Boundaries of Mind, Body, and Soul*. York Beach, ME: Samuel Weiser, 2000.

*Thomas, William H. *What Are Old People For? How Elders Will Save the World.* Acton, MA: Vanderwyk and Burnham, 2004.

Tompkins, Mark L. and Jennifer McMahan, eds. *Illuminations: Expressions of the Personal Spiritual Experience.* Berkeley, CA: Celestial Arts, 2006.

Tudge, Colin. *The Tree: A Natural History of What Trees Are, How They Live, and Why They Matter.* NYC: Crown, 2006.

University of California Los Angeles. "UCLA Researchers Identify Key Biobehavioral Pattern Used By Women To Manage Stress." *Science Daily,* 22 May 2000. 11 December 2007. http://www.sciencedaily.com/releases/2000/05/000522082151.htm.

U.S. Department of Labor, Bureau of Labor Statistics. "Women in the Labor Force: A Databook," U.S. Department of Labor, May 2005, Report 985, http://www.bls.gov/cps/wlf-intro-2005.pdf.

Volk, Tyler. *Metapatterns: Across Space, Time, and Mind.* NYC: Columbia University Press, 1995.

Waldfogel, Joel. "The Midlife Happiness Crisis." *Slate.Com,* 16 Mar. 2007.

Weiss, Robert S. *The Experience of Retirement.* Ithaca, NY: Cornell University Press, 2005.

*Whyte, David. *Crossing the Unknown Sea: Work as a Pilgrimage of Identity.* NYC: Riverhead Books, 2001.

Zemke, Ron, Claire Raines, and Bob Filipczak. *Generations At Work: Managing the Clash of Veterans, Boomers, Xers, and Nexters in Your Workplace.* NYC: American Management Assoc., 2000.

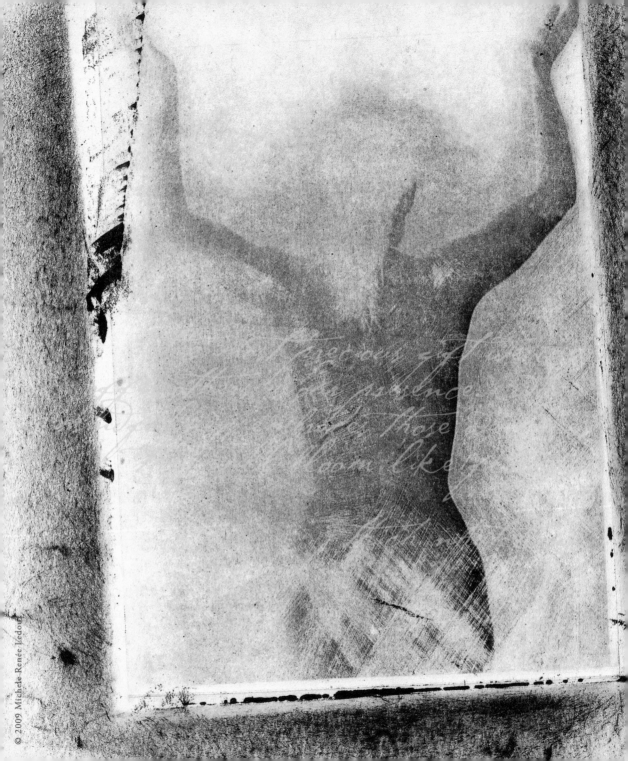

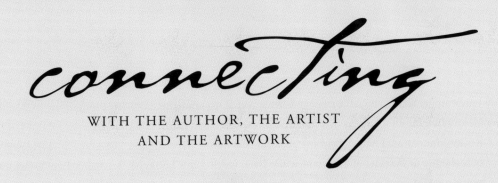

connecting

WITH THE AUTHOR, THE ARTIST
AND THE ARTWORK

"… our work is to come home to ourselves and discover where we are truly content, happy, and satisfied…. where deep self-acceptance resides and where we trust our natural being and our inner wilderness. The most splendid external expression of that wilderness is nature itself. Nature in its majestic beauty can put our soul at ease, relax us, and deliver us to a timeless mystery that opens the doors to contemplation, reflection, integration, and transformation. When we experience inner quiet and peacefulness, we can savor the wisdom and spirituality found in nature, in silence, and in precious moments we experience at the center of our being." *Angeles Arrien* (149)

"The most precious gift we can offer others is our presence. When mindfulness embraces those we love, they will bloom like flowers. *Thich Nhat Hanh*

Deborah F Windrum

I grew up in Southern California, and my career as an academic librarian brought me to Boulder, Colorado in 1980. Here, at this juncture of the semi-arid plains and pine-covered foothills of the Rocky Mountains, I have found my geo-spiritual home. My daughter joined me at the University of Colorado at Boulder as a student while I was writing this book. My husband, Bart Windrum, president of Axiom Action LLC, published in 2008 the award-winning book, *Notes from the Waiting Room: Managing a Loved One's End-of-Life Hospitalization*, leading the way for our on-going publishing ventures.

My career has enriched and informed my life in many ways. Since my passions arise from learning, opportunities I've had to recreate my position have kept me in the same place, if not the same intellectual space, for nearly three decades. I joined the University of Colorado at Boulder Libraries faculty in 1980 to coordinate instructional services, and transitioned to public information in 1990 and then to campus relations and outreach in 2002.

I trace my "career path" by conceptual rather than traditional advances. Early on at the University Libraries I began to perceive libraries and information in a broader context that mirrors social issues rather than transcending them. My enjoyment of teaching and love of learning led me to an exploration of learning styles and approaches for creating interactive learning environments. I developed a national model for a research skills course based on those perspectives, which was published by the American Library Association in 1989.

Together with Abbie Loomis, a colleague at UW-Madison, I created the concept of "meta-learning," and we presented workshops for librarians nationally in the early 1990s. In the mid-1990s, I became an independent PhotoReading instructor and contract workshop facilitator for Learning Strategies Corporation, whose Whole Mind Reading System remains life-changing for me.

I now enjoy creating *intra*-active publications and events for women who are experiencing the mature prime of their life as an inner and outer adventure in the richness of aging. I originated and co-facilitate *Over the Moon Ovations*, a monthly gathering of women in the second half of life sponsored by the Boulder Public Library. I also consult with others interested in initiating similar gatherings in their community.

Having coined the term "meta-liminal" to describe the conscious life stage transitioning of women willing to live from their inner knowing and acceptance of death as an honoring of life, I am now creating the web-based resource OMyHarvestMoon.com.

The Harvest Moon, or full moon rising closest to the autumn equinox, is distinctive for its brightness tinted with the coloration of the season. It acquired its name because the length of time between sunset and moonrise is shorter in the autumn, reducing the interval between the provision of illumination from celestial light givers and providing early farmers the opportunity to continue working into the evening at the height of their harvesting season.

For women today in the second half of life, long attuned to lunar cycles through menses and our sensitivity to natural rhythms, the Harvest Moon is a distinctive symbol of new opportunities for continued enterprise late into our autumn season of life. And like the Harvest Moon itself, women enjoying maturity serve others by shining our light—recognizing that we are beautiful in our own right.

I facilitate half-day, day-long, and multi-session "retreats" on Harvest the Bounty of Your Career, Harvest Your Mid-Life Bounty, Resources for Your Harvest Moon, Cultivate Your Inner Wise Woman, The Four-Part Harmony of a Woman's Life Cycle, and any related theme or topic.

I also deliver eclectic and integrative keynote presentations. Described as an engaging and inspiring presenter with a heart-based, yet polished, style, I will set a positive and lively tone for your meeting, event, or conference.

Please visit www.OMyHarvestMoon.com.

artist

Michele Renée Ledoux

"Ledoux feels the impulsive desire to stop realities and objects belonging to quotidian images, filling them with magic, rarified, lyric effects and revealing to us details of a nature soaked with poetical aspects that often slip from us.... [Her] artwork reveals secrets. Not only her eye, but her soul and spirit unharness Truth, Wisdon, Life and Passion. She discloses what natural and human made objects wait for others to embrace." Paola Trevisan, Art Critic, Italy

Through various forms of mixed media including photography, written word and painting, my work aims to reveal our original source—a peeling back, if you will, to reveal our deepest truth. By means of building up and breaking down, revealing, texturing, and layering, my work seeks to scratch the surface of true human nature resulting in the conclusion that we are, in fact, all the same.

I continue to share my work and passion in numerous group and solo exhibitions across the United States and internationally. Locally, I have served as the creative director for a community-based, positive-news-only newspaper and continue to work as a freelance artist, graphic designer, and creative consultant. Cofounder of the creative consulting firm, *Art As Endless Possibility* (www.artasendlesspossibility.com), I am wholly rooted in my commitment to the creation of an open, organic and intimate approach to *all* creative endeavors. Additionally, I am a proactive participant and consultant for a variety of local arts events, humanitarian projects and inspirational publications in and around the Evergreen, Colorado area.

Please visit www.mledoux.com to view my online portfolio.

Artist statement for "alchemy of align" body of work featured in this book

"It [Alchemy] is about penetrating to the Soul of the World, and discovering the treasure that has been reserved for you." Paulo Coelho, *The Alchemist*

"[A]lchemy of align" is a uniquely organic collection of work that focuses on the common thread that connects us all. Weaving together several innovative techniques including printmaking, painting, drawing, and photography, each image intends to provoke the viewer to rediscover the profound nature of alchemy—the transmutation of the mundane into magic.

Magic. It's all around us. It's in us. It is us. It requires no rational explanation. It ignites our innate ability to transform our life experiences into pure joy. It is our "gold." And, as such, we need not be in search of a universal elixir. We are the elixir. We are the line... the line that connects us to our eternal source. And, if we simply allow, the line will take us anywhere we want to go.

"You can't hide anything in a line. You are there whatever line you draw. And you will stay there, even when you go somewhere else. If your personality is interesting enough, the line will be interesting. To do this, you have to be fearless." Kazuaki Tanahashi, *Brush Mind*

There are no mistakes. There are only gifts.

Please visit www.alchemyofalign.com to view this ongoing body of work.

Featured Artwork

"attunement" monotype, chin collé, painting on paper | 16" x 16" | cover*

Representing the harmonious mingling of all elements, "attunement" draws upon the form of the cross for inspiration. In this way, its very nature is indicative of the human desire to know and experience the unfolding mystery of life. One can actually feel the sensation of oneness, wholeness and unity in its form.

"seasoned in olive" monotype, chin collé, scratching painting on paper | 22" x 8" | cover/back flap/bookmark*

Speaking to the wisdom that lies within each of us, "seasoned in olive" shifts our vision and appreciation of beauty.

"guiding stillness" monotype, chin collé, painting on paper | 16" x 12" | pi

Elegant and centered, "guiding stillness" reminds us that it is our inner voice that guides us on the Way.

"untitled" monotype on newsprint | 8" x 10" | piii

"steadfast and wavering" monotype, chin collé, scratching painting on paper | 22" x 8" | toc, pv*

Inviting the viewer to appreciate the beauty that surrounds us all, "steadfast and wavering" opens our hearts and minds to the seeming paradox of life itself.

"a cup of tea, green" pottery, monotype, chin collé, collage, painting on paper | 19¼" x 8¼" | pviii

"[C]up of tea, green" is a tribute to the open invitation to conversation, learning and sharing experienced while enjoying a cup of tea among friends. It also references the well-known koan from "101 Zen Stories"—a 1919 compilation of Zen koans including 19th and early 20th century anecdotes, and Collection of Stone and Sand, written in the 13th century by Japanese Zen master Muju.

"abstract with overtones" monotype, painting on paper | 16" x 16" | p8

"[A]bstract with overtones" suggests the profound nature of a horizon set upon the layers of energetic resonance that breathe with the earth as it exposes its potential. This horizon line joins earth and sky and presents the viewer with a barren, yet not so barren landscape on which to create their own experience.

"unearthed potential in orange" monotype, chin collé, collage, painting on paper | 16" x 16" | p18*

"[U]nearthed potential in orange" draws upon the notion that each and every one of our thoughts, words and actions begins with a seed. These seeds are experienced by the earth energetically not only as a part, but also as the whole, and each one manifests only when we choose to open to the infinite potential of all that is.

"rising fire" monotype, chin collé, collage, painting, scratching, drawing on paper | 16" x 12" | p26

Drawing on the triangle as the alchemical symbol for fire, "rising fire" speaks to the creative spark that lies within us all. Much like the Native American ceremony of raising a teepee, "rising fire" is a celebration and honoring of the fact that is only by allowing our fire to rise inside of us that we find our true creative purpose.

"sourcing alignment" monotype, chin collé, painting, scratching on paper | 16" x 16" | p35

In order to align ourselves with our highest potential so that we may self-actualize, we must source the whole of our life experience. "[S]ourcing alignment, bittersweet" showcases the intimate connection that we, as spiritual beings having a material experience, create and experience with our environment each and every day. Representing the interconnectedness of the life cycle, the tree not only reaches up to the sun and sky in an open exchange of energy, but also extends itself deep into the earth to pull from the roots of its experiences and "source its own alignment."

"the way tree" monotype, chin collé, collage, painting, scratching on paper | 16" x 12" | p42*

Also drawing on the sacred symbol of the cross, "the way tree" presents itself as symbolic compass, guiding us through a spiritual sea in which the cross serves as a stable guidepost that always leads us to our "true north." The central tree photograph, taken on the Camino de Santiago, contains a yellow arrow in its trunk. This arrow serves as a guide for pilgrims on their 500-mile journey to Santiago de Compostela, the home of St. James and the conclusion of the pilgrimage. The arrow is also the symbol for the rune of the spiritual warrior and, as such, calls us to strengthen our resolve to align the self with the Self. A rune of inward looking, "Teiwaz" asks us to delve down to the foundations of life so as to meet the deepest needs of our nature and tap into our most profound resources.

"rooted in bleu" monotype, chin collé, collage, painting, scratching on paper | 16" x 12" | p51

"[R]ooted in bleu" juxtaposes the nourishing qualities and life force of water with the preconceived notion that roots must be a certain color or structure. It also makes reference to the wealth of sustenance available to us all when we truly tap our own potential.

"unexpected visitor" monotype, chin collé, collage, painting, drawing on paper | 16" x 16" | p60

"[U]nexpected visitor" extends an invitation to view the symbiotic relationship between the tree and all of its many helpers. In this work, the tree reaches out in friendship to a bird, which represents the freedom of flight, thus embracing the cycle of life.

"cede to whim" monotype, chin collé, painting, drawing on paper | 16" x 16" | p76

"[C]ede to whim" beckons the reader to recognize the playful nature of the journey of the fruit/seed on its path of discovery. At the same time, it invites us to consider unleashing our own playful freedom as we travel on our many life paths.

"the opening" monotype, chin collé, painting, scratching on paper | 16" x 12" | p87

"[T]he opening" speaks directly to the flowering of the soul that occurs once we choose to cultivate our inner gardens by aligning our selves with source.

"feathered muse" monotype, chin collé, collage, painting, drawing on paper | 16" x 16" | p94

And so the "feathered muse" whispers sweet nothings upon the pod of life.

"silent muse" monotype, chin collé, collage, painting, drawing on paper | 16" x 16" | p104

Even amidst the "silent muse," the seeds of life present themselves with great joy.

"the gathering" monotype, chin collé, painting, drawing on paper | 16" x 12" | p110

In open fields, we gather to grow—"the gathering."

"portal thru which" monotype, chin collé, painting, on paper | 16" x 12" | p120

"[P]ortal thru which" connects two mirrored teepee images as they each sit on a horizon line sharing sky and root deeply to the earth both above and below. The opening that is created by the joining of these two triangles (one symbolizing fire and the other water) is the portal thru which one must leap in order to embrace the unknown and grow.

"coming into tree pose" monotype, chin collé, scratching and painting on paper | 30" x 22" | p130

Tree Pose is one of the foundational yoga postures for increasing balance. Much like the yoga pose, "coming into tree pose" invites us to explore the many energetic patterns that must come into alignment in order to create balance in our lives.

"fertile passage" monotype, chin collé, scratching and painting on paper | 19¼" x 8¼" | p150

The passage to self-actualization is indeed lined by our tall choices.

"fertile passage" [abstraction] monotype, chin collé, scratching and painting on paper | 19¼" x 8¼" | p151*

"untitled" monotype on newsprint | 8" x 10" | p176

Artwork has been modified from its original state for the purposes of this book.

spiraling...

I trust that the tree and season metaphors have proven as rich and fulfilling for you as they have for me. I hope that each chapter herein has offered affirmation, challenge, fresh perspective, and new ideas lifting you to yet another round of your own personal spiral.

It is now dark outside my window—the apple tree almost invisible. If we close our eyes, we can see with our inner minds the glistening tree I pointed out to you when we started our visit.

We can picture the abundant fruit—vessels of precious seeds—and imagine the deep roots invisibly sustaining the venerable trunk and spreading branches. Like us, the tree is fulfilling a cycle of life. And she is a muse to me. As I contemplate my own future stage of life as Muse, I discover how thrilled I am at the prospect of becoming a Wise Woman. Imagine us in the future sharing a specially brewed pot of tea and conjuring a fresh vision for being the Wise Women our world is yearning for...

happy growing!

Deb